AF490637

TO BUILD A RED STATE NATION

The GOP, The Electoral College, and The Path to save the American Republic from the Left.

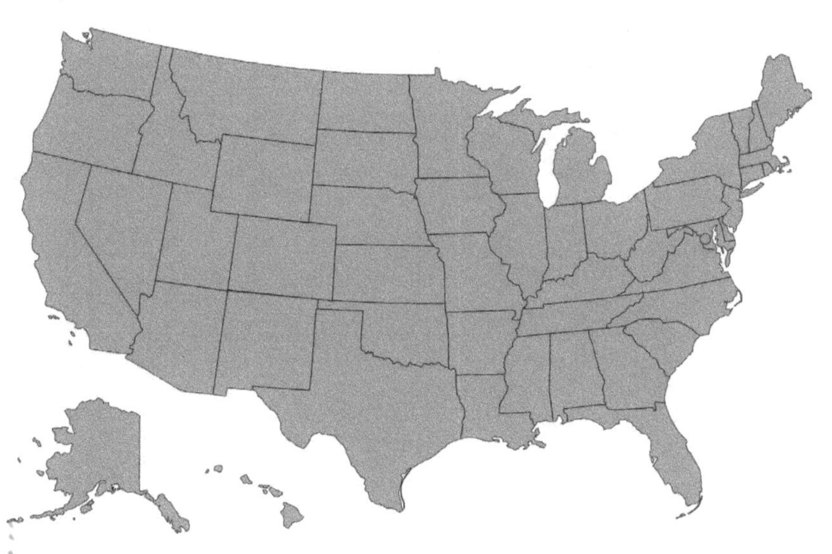

GEORGE W. ELLIS

Copyright © 2024, George W. Ellis

All rights reserved.

No part of this publication may be reproduced, stored in a retrieval system or transmitted in any form or by any means, electronic, mechanical, photocopying, recording or otherwise, without prior written permission from the publisher.

Paperback ISBN : 979-8-9907782-0-7
eBook ISBN : 979-8-9907782-1-4

CONTENTS

CHAPTER 1:

THE 2008, 2012, 2016
PRESIDENTIAL ELECTIONS: AN OVERVIEW.

On November 4, 2008, Democratic candidate, Illinois US Senator, Barrack Hussein Obama won the Presidential election in significant fashion winning 28 states with a total of 365 Electoral votes, while Republican candidate, Arizona US Senator John McCain, won 22 states with a total of 173 Electoral votes. In the popular vote, Obama collected 66,882,230 popular votes for a percentage of 53% while McCain collected 58,343,671 popular votes for a percentage of 46%.

In the 2012 Presidential election, Republican candidate Mitt Romney opposing Barack Obama's re-election effort performed marginally better than did McCain in his 2008 effort. Romney in 2012 won 206 electoral votes, holding Obama to 332 electoral votes. Romney also won an approximate 5% of the African-American vote (up from McCain's 4% in 2008). Romney's portion of the Caucasian vote however in 2012 did rise to an approximate 72%, up from McCain's 57% in 2008. In addition, Romney's portion of the Hispanic vote dipped to only 27% in 2012 (down from McCain's 31% in 2008). Donald Trump's winning GOP effort in 2016 was distinguished by both significant improvement from both McCain's and Romney's earlier efforts winning a total of 31 states, 306 electoral votes, approximately 8% of the African-American vote, and 32% of the Hispanic vote. He did however lose the popular vote by an excess of 2 million votes+ to 2016 Democratic candidate, Hillary Clinton, amidst reports that much of Clinton's winning margin of popular votes came from the voting of illegal aliens, in a number of states, particularly California. Illegal-alien voting, in American elections-primarily encouraged by and benefiting Democrats, especially in Presidential elections-goes far to the purpose of this work to call for a Red State Nation. I shall discuss much more about this later.

Obama's 2008 electoral victory was clearly significant with potential critical consequences for America's future. Nationally, Obama won approximately 96% of the African-American vote. He also won approximately 69% of the overall Hispanic vote with variations in specific states such as Florida), and a very healthy 43% of the overall Caucasian vote as well. These numbers should and must give serious pause and concern to all Republican-oriented voters in this country, and most particularly to those millions of conservatives. For conservatives who believe in personal freedom; are opposed to unchecked omniscient government; who cherish this nation's Judeo-Christian heritage; who wish to resist this nation's turn towards European-style socialism which Obama's election represents; and who wish to preserve this nation's free enterprise economic system-the time for action and to get involved in the attempt to preserve this nation's future-is now! We can delay no longer.

If the United States is to remain a model of a free-enterprise economy and not one of pro-European socialism, it will only be through the energetic efforts of American conservatives and their allies in the Republican Party. Conservatives and committed Republicans are the country's last best hope to insure that this nation itself remains the last best hope to the masses of the rest of the world as both a beacon of light and symbol of freedom. It is an ironic symbolism implicit within Obama's election as an image to the rest of the world since Obama himself as an African-American is such a symbol, and his election seemingly verifies America's symbolism as a nation which represents freedom and opportunity.

However, while Obama's election as an African-American man does verify America's symbolic image to the rest of the world, his leftist, socialist, Pro-European ideology actually repudiates the concepts of freedom, self-reliance, and opportunity. Obama's election and governance as well as the continued election of additional Democratic Presidents following him who share his leftist, socialist views will spell the death knell of the America as we have known it; that of the free and open society of opportunity which had allowed Obama to prosper and succeed in the first place.

Beyond the Obama Presidency, and if his Presidency is followed by that of successive Democratic Presidents who follow a leftist, socialistic agenda similar to-and a continuation of-Obama's own-the possible consequences are grave and will ultimately result in an America that will in 20 or 30 years be scarcely recognizable to us today. The flight of American capital-and capitalists-overseas to favorable and less taxing shores-already in evidence today, will become a process greatly accelerated into possible flood proportions. Capital like water due to its inherent nature seeks the path of least resistance. Much capital had already fled the country by the end of Obama's tenure in 2016. One of the main plans of the incoming President Trump's program was to lure this errant capital back into the country to fuel growth by attractive non-Obama type confiscatory tax policies. We have seen enough demographic evidence to support this idea in recent American history. Look at the many thousands of Americans who in recent years have migrated from the higher tax states of the Northern United States (and especially New York) to the lower tax states in the Southern United States as especially Florida, as well as others.

Lower energy and real estate costs are also a significant factor for many of these people to relocate South as well. Even within states, this process of the flight of capital-and of its productive tax-paying owners-has clearly been in evidence. Take for example the city of Philadelphia, Pennsylvania in which for most of the 20" Century -Philadelphia had steadily continued to shed productive middle-class residents, and tax base, due to its high city tax structure. Philadelphia is in fact one of the highest taxed cities in the United States. In the years from 1950 to 2000, Philadelphia has lost 554, 055 residents (a net loss of 26.7% total population) -a large percentage of those who left being productive, tax-paying, middle class residents; the type of residents a struggling city can ill afford to lose.

Philadelphia is hardly alone, however. All over the United States, many thousands of productive middle class and tax paying citizens-and across all racial lines-have fled most of our larger cities including Detroit, Boston, Chicago, Washington, D.C., New York, Los Angeles, etc. for both high tax as well as quality of life issues. With New York City and its various Republican mayors over the years (i.e.. Lindsay, Guiliani, Bloomberg) as the glaring exceptions, virtually all of these other cities have experienced consistent one-party left-wing, Democratic rule for many years with the end result of that being that they all have experienced job loss, population loss, and tax base loss as most of their productive middle class and tax paying residents who possessed the means and resources to flee, have done so, leaving the urban poor and lower middle class behind.

Now the United States as a whole primarily due to the merging of a very unique set of circumstances in the 2008 Presidential election year: the great unpopularity of outgoing Republican President, George W. Bush; plus, that of the Iraq War to which he was intractably committed to; plus, the country's many and serious economic problems coming to a flash point at the same time-the country elected as President, Barack Hussein Obama.

Now in Obama, the United States had elected as president a President with a left-wing political agenda-arguably even a socialist one-more extreme for the time than that possessed by anyone elected US President. What will be the reaction to Obama's election-particularly if as feared-his election is immediately followed by other Presidents with an extreme Democratic left-wing agenda due to both a philosophical as well as a demographic shift within the US electorate? Regardless of such a shift, 58 million Americans-the vast majority of them being Caucasian-did vote against Obama in the 2008 Presidential election. As we have already seen in the middle-class flight from the various large cities in this country with their one-party leftist Democratic Party rule, how many Americans with the means to do so, are now going to leave the United States-or at least contemplate doing so-to escape Obama's one-party leftist/socialist rule, or a subsequent Democratic President, equally ideologically extreme?

And if Obama's Presidency-and Trump's- is again followed by other left-wing Democratic Presidents, will a trickle of conservative, (primarily) Caucasian, middle- and upper-class Americans fleeing Obama's Presidency for places such as Canada, Mexico, various Central American countries, Brazil, Cayman Islands, Australia, New Zealand, Spain, Portugal, France, England, etc. become a flood? If so, the slow but steady march of the United States into a primarily non-white and third-world nation will greatly accelerate.

Based upon the results of the 2008 Presidential election and the victory of Barack Hussein Obama and the sobering demographics which greatly contributed to it, America's future as I have just painted it if the present demographic trends continue in our national elections, is clearly not an attractive one. If conservative Republican candidates can no longer win national elections for President, then the United States will degenerate into a one-party nation state in which the one ruling party-the Democratic Party-will run and elect a succession of leftist and socialist candidates for President, and in which the factor determining a particular candidates election will primarily be one of personality, and not ideology.

Even if the point is reached that conservatives and Republicans can no longer win national Presidential elections, they can still politically control certain states-primarily situated in the South, Mid-West, and Far West-and thus maintain a degree of check or control on the actions of the ruling Democratic Party and its leader, and thus create a degree of check or control on the actions of the ruling Democratic Party and its leaders, and to create the situation wherein certain instances, the Republicans will have to be brokered with to achieve a particular political objective. This "Red State Veto" consensus or scenario as I would term it (for lack of an apparent better one) is a scenario that could-and would-last only as long as the Republicans world politically control a sufficient number of "Red States" to continue the scenario as an effective check on the power of the Democrats.

What would likely erode the political power of the Republicans to control the sufficient number of "Red States" to continue to wield the "veto" is the exodus of conservative and Republican voters from the Red States, and from the nation as well. Present many conservative and Republican voters with the prospect that they and their ideas will no longer prevail in national political elections and that the best that they could hope for is simply a limited veto power over the actions of the ruling Democrats, then what is the incentive for conservatives to remain in the country-particularly for those who possess the means to leave? The continued national elections of Democrats to rule in Washington, D.C. with their agenda for socialism and confiscatory taxation-if unchecked-should certainly fuel continued exodus of conservatives.

The demographic statistics which explain and support Barack Hussein Obama's 2008 election to the Presidency are quite sobering and cause for great concern from a conservative perspective. Obama won the election by winning approximately 96% of the African-American vote; 69% of the Hispanic vote; and 43% of the Caucasian vote. Since the African-American and especially the Hispanic population in the United States is growing at a much faster rate than is the white population, within the next 20-30 years the United States will become a majority non-white nation. Since the present white majority of this nation is facing a rapidly-approaching minority status-and since the Republican Party has always been a Caucasian party as well-its continued national minority status is assured with the prospective gloomy scenarios that I've already painted, unless the Party takes serious measure of the 2008 election results as a wake-up call.

What can and must be done? Both the Republican Party as a whole and the millions of loyal voters, members, and volunteers who have always supported the Party and its various litany of conservative causes over the years must properly and realistically face the future, and the significant demographic changes now going on within this country-and those still yet to come-of which Obama's 2008 election was just a warning bell.

A somewhat accurate analogy might be that the white Republican and conservative voters collectively are like a surfer sitting in the ocean on their surfboard watching the slow, yet steadily-approaching giant wave coming straight at them. In a real situation, a surfer could duck under the wave, or perhaps swim to shore. Conservatives in this country do not have the option of swimming to shore with the gathering demographic wave that we now face. We can allow this wave to swamp us to permanent minority-party status with the increasingly grim portrait for both us and the socialistic future of this country which that alternative signifies as I have already shown.

In the alternative, conservatives can choose to ride this demographic wave of change by skillfully managing it. Conservatives can-and must-do a much better job of expanding our outreach into the African-American and particularly the Hispanic communities in this country to seek our like-minded conservatives in these communities, and to encourage these minority community conservatives to join common cause with us to preserve this nation from leftist socialism-especially so in the Hispanic community. We now have no choice but to do so with the very real prospect of 2 class or minority political membership now facing us.

The largest single demographic difference from the 2004 Presidential election results when Republican candidate, President George W. Bush won re-election, to the 2008 election results when Republican candidate, John McCain lost was the reduction in the percentage of the Hispanic vote from the 44% won by Bush in 2004, to the 31% won by McCain in 2008. Many knowledgeable national political observers such as Karl Rove, President Bush's former advisor and 2004 and 2008 Presidential campaign chairman, do not believe that the Republican Party can win national elections any longer without significantly increasing its percentage of the Hispanic vote from the 31% won by McCain in 2008 to a consistent percentage much closer to the 44% won by President Bush in 2004. I concur with this conclusion by Karl Rove.

I particularly concur when one recognizes that not only will the overall percentage of the Hispanic vote in the total electorate will rise because the Hispanic rate in population growth is faster than that for Caucasian people, but that a compromise may finally be reached to possibly extend a path to citizenship to those Hispanics who originally entered the country illegally. If that event occurs, not only will the percentage of potential Hispanic voters be greatly increased, but undoubtedly many of these new potential Hispanic voters will express their gratitude for the newly-won path to citizenship by registering and voting Democratic.

The dramatic reduction in the percentage of Republican Hispanic voters from 2004 to 2008 was a direct cause in the Republican loss in the 2008 John McCain campaign of several states-some reliably Republican ones-that President Bush won in 2004. These states included: Nevada, Colorado, New Mexico, Florida, Virginia, North Carolina, and Indiana. Republicans and conservatives cannot just surrender the Hispanic vote to the Democrats, and they must fight the Democrats tooth and nail for every Hispanic voter just as any other. We cannot allow the Democrats to gain the inside track with Hispanics and Hispanic voters, even on the "Path to Citizenship" As evidenced by their voting behavior in the past, many Hispanics are philosophically oriented to vote for the GOP in any event as they share many of the same family and conservative values as do typically, nominal Republican voters. Many Hispanics are the product of- and believe in-strong family units. Many of them work-and hard-and pay their taxes. Many of them are industrious-and are self-employed. Many of them are religious-and regularly attend church.

In short, American Hispanics as a whole are far too valuable and compatible an electoral ally to simply abandon to the Democratic Party. In contrast, the great mass of African-American voters are philosophically much more attuned to the Democratic Party with its socialistic agenda and welfare state mentality, particularly if the Democratic Party attempts in future national elections to duplicate its electoral success in 2008 with Obama by recruiting and nominating African-American candidates for President.

The Republican Party's prospects to attract African-American support in much greater numbers than the consistently low single digits than it attracted in 2008 did not at one time appear promising unless the Party took a very serious measure of the 2008 Election results as a wake-up call, which they ultimately did under the leadership of RNC Chairman, Reince Priebus of Wisconsin in the form of a greatly expanded minority outreach program. In addition, the percentage of the African-American portion of the total population is growing, just as the African-American population-like the Hispanic-is growing faster than the Caucasian population. President Trump, newly elected in 2016, opposed to the concept of a pathway to citizenship extended to those Hispanics and other nationalities who entered the country illegally, butting in front of those from other countries who entered the country legally, and who are patiently trying to secure American citizenship in the legal, traditional manner. It has been widely reported that President Obama have greatly exploited the presence in the country of millions of illegal immigrants by registering them to vote-and by illegally having them vote Democratic in the various states in the 2008, 2012, and 2016 Presidential, and other elections. This has been widely reported to have happened in the states of New Mexico, Arizona, Florida, Nevada, Colorado, New York, and especially California (in very large numbers).

Free fair, and democratic elections cannot occur when one political party exploit's the voting process by enlisting the votes to support their party of otherwise unqualified and fraudulent voters who are not legal US citizens as they entered the country, illegally. President Obama and the Democratic Party seek to exploit the voting potential of the millions of illegal immigrants in the country by overwhelming in numbers the Republican votes of lawful American citizens. The goal of the Democrats in doing this of course, is to essentially make free, fair elections meaningless; to insure that the Democrats win every election-particularly the national ones-and that the United States in effect, becomes a one-party nation state under the perpetual control of the Democratic Party and their illegal alien voters. The Republican Party can in turn, concentrate its electoral strength and power by the Red State Nation concept which is the subject of this effort. Republicans must abandon especially those hard-blue states like California, New York, Illinois, etc. and the others where they are greatly outnumbered by the Democrats and their illegal immigrant allies. Republicans must instead concentrate in numbers and political strength in both the hard-red states like Indiana, Kentucky, and Tennessee, and also purple states like Pennsylvania, Ohio, and Virginia, and in so doing, flip these states from purple to red. The most effective counter to the efforts of the Democratic Party to transform the United States into a blue-state controlled nation via its swamping the country with voting illegal immigrants and foreign refugees is to in turn transform the nation into a red state nation through the voting efforts-both in the ballot box and by their feet-of patriotic American GOP and conservatives.

Overall, African-Americans' shared socialistic and welfare state ideals with those of the national Democratic Party; coupled with popular African-American enthusiasm and support for liberal Democratic African-American candidates such as Obama gives rise to the expectation that Obama's success all but insures that such candidates will continue. This is evidenced by the example of former US Army General and Secretary of State, Colin Powell, an African-American and previously self-identified Republican, and his support for

Obama's candidacy in 2008. This in turn all but insures that African-American support for national Republican candidates could continue to be insignificant for the foreseeable future, although President Trump's determination to attract black voters to the GOP is most encouraging.

The major emphasis then for the Republican Party in national elections must be to maximize Hispanic as well as all other non-African-American minority support in order to compete in future national elections. The Republican party should strive to attain in all national elections a consistent minimal percentage of 40% of the Hispanic vote. If this percentage is consistently reached, the Republican Party should be quite competitive in all national elections. Increased African-American support for the GOP via President Trump's efforts would be so much the better.

CHAPTER 2:

AMERICA 2016;
A NATION AT THE CROSSROADS.

Barack Hussein Obama campaigned for President in 2008 on a theme of change, and there is little doubt that with the event of his election as President that this country has indeed changed. But how exactly has it changed? There is little doubt that to Obama's millions of gleeful supporters, his election represents a positive change for the United States. But what of those-such as myself-who did not support-or vote for Obama-and to whom the advent of his election represents significant change, yes, of a much more uncertain kind as to what it really means, and of whether it is positive change or not?

And of course, there are millions in the United States who did not support or vote for Obama, and who were greatly troubled, and fearful of his election as President, and of the significant change that did follow. I shared many of those feelings of concern and trepidation as to the nature and extent of the changes that are apparently accompanying the election of Obama. Now I see the awakening of a new militancy by both atheists and gay activists; and of course, that of the other far-left elements of the Obama coalition as they stridently demanded the rapid implementation of Obama's socialist agenda during his entire 8-year tenure

I am but an observer of these episodes of "change" heralded in by Obama's election and I feel almost a distinct disconnect from this, my country, the United States of America, and I question my place and appropriate role in this, Obama's nation of "change," and I really wonder if this is my country anymore. With Obama's election-and recognizing that in electing Obama-America emphatically rejected a legitimate hero-John McCain-to do so, I even now look differently at the American flag. How can one, I ask, look at the American flag as a symbol the same way that I previously did when in electing Obama as President, we have elected a President who for 20 years sat in a church as a congregant of a minister who was heard angrily to exclaim in a taped sermon: "God Damn America!"

Also, it is the same American flag that another one of Obama's friends and political advisors-a 1960's bomb-making radical and current Leftist college professor-and who was in recent years, photographed standing on it. Who are the true guardians of this nation, its flag, and all that both previously represented-Obama and his extreme friends and associates who have made a career of tearing down this nation and its flag, or those millions of conservatives such as myself who opposed Obama-though admittedly lost-but did so with the intention to both preserve the nation, its flag, and all that both heretofore, represented? Yes, whose nation and flag is this anymore? With Obama's election, America truly was a nation in the wilderness; a nation at the crossroads in 2008. However, the nation did survive the rule of Obama and the Left.

I liken American Presidential elections every 4 years between Democratic and Republican candidates as similar to a military campaign, or perhaps at least a chess match. The Presidential election winner must accumulate a minimum of 270 electoral votes in the Electoral College of a total of 538 electoral votes distributed among all 50 states, plus the District of Columbia. As part of the effort to reclaim elective leadership in the nation-and to permanently retain it-the Republican and conservative leadership in the nation must look at-plus utilize-the Electoral College "map" as the strategic tool that it is. The Electoral College 'map" is the chessboard or the battlefield in our ongoing war with the Democratic, socialist left to lead and control this nation.

As evidenced by the meltdown of the Bush Presidency throughout its 2nd Term from 2005-2008-plus that of the fortunes of the Republican Party along with it-all leading of course to Obama's election-the conservatives and the Republican Party in this country are not winning this war, although we should be. On issue after issue, public opinion polls routinely demonstrate that the United States is a reliably right-of-center nation. Obama himself is certainly cognizant of this fact by several of his actions and pronouncements both prior to his Inauguration, and in the early days of his Presidency. Candidate Obama in the 2008 campaign, certainly was presented and packaged as a far more agreeable and conservative sounding candidate, than President Obama ultimately proved to be throughout his entire Presidency.

National elections every four years are merely battles in the ongoing war for control of this country between conservatives and the Democratic left. The national conservative and Republican leadership in this country must move beyond the limited-and problematical-goal of simply attempting to win elections every four years to the larger goal of attempting to win the entire war for political control of this country with the Democratic left by properly using the Electoral College "map" as the strategic tool or benchmark that it is. If this expanded strategy of fighting-and winning-the ongoing political war with the Democratic left is adopted and followed, Republican and conservative success in national elections every four years would take care of itself.

How should the ongoing war with the Democratic left be continued as a national strategy with the utilizing of the Electoral College "map" as a strategic tool? It is very easy to see-and as always-conservatives themselves control the key. As one can see from the results of the last several Presidential elections, Democrats count on the Electoral Votes as keys to national victory from the same large and reliably "Blue" states, election after election. Just the four states of California, New York, Illinois, and New Jersey-which almost always vote for the Democratic candidate in Presidential elections-by themselves constitute approximately 46% of the 270 Electoral Votes necessary to win the White House. These four states are large with millions of voters, and in which within each one-within no exceptions-contain many thousands-and in the case perhaps of California and New York-millions of reliably loyal conservative and Republican voters.

These loyal conservative and Republican voters in these four states-while numerous-are unfortunately not numerous enough, particularly in Presidential Election years to swing the state for the Republican candidate, given the even more significant and preponderant number of leftists and Democratic voters in these states-especially New York and California. As can be evidenced then by the example of these four states which contribute so significantly to Democratic national electoral victory when successful, as it was in the case of Obama's in 2008, conservative Republican votes in leftist Democratic states are self-defeating and accomplish nothing other than tighten the chains of leftist socialism ever tighter around us all. Millions of Republican and conservative votes in both the 2008 Presidential election-as well as the previous several Presidential elections in the four states of California, New York, New Jersey, and Illinois-accomplished nothing beneficial for the conservative cause in this country and served only in each instance to inflate the Electoral Vote total of the respective losing Democratic Presidential candidates, or in the case of the 2008 election, the winning one, Barack Hussein Obama.

How can loyal conservative voters and taxpayers in these four states in particular-but in general, anywhere-continue to live, work, worship, and especially-vote, in a state where their conservative values are not recognized-and indeed are frequently mocked-and whose hard-earned tax dollars are frequently wasted on socialistic programs invented and administered by leftist technocrats? How can conservatives in California continue to live and pay taxes in a state where they are represented by the likes of Barbara Boxer and Diane Finestein as US Senators, plus also Nancy Pelosi as a US Representative, and a state whose values are dictated by the latest trends in vogue in radical San Francisco, as well as those favored by the leftist Hollywood elite? California also being a state where millions of illegal immigrants are permitted to reside, unchallenged.; not pay taxes; use a disproportionate share of social services which legitimate taxpayers-mostly Republicans-pay for.

Also, California is a state where illegal immigrants are permitted to obtain drivers licenses which then can be utilized to register to vote, illegal or not. And as evidenced by the voting figures in the 2016 Presidential Election, millions of illegal immigrants in California evidently did vote-the vast majority voting Democratic, of course. California in summary is an intolerable situation-or should be-to the typical conservative working GOP taxpayer who resides there and is used to playing by the rules. Lastly, and perhaps the ultimate insult, California's Democratic majority legislature announced shortly after Donald Trump's victory in the 2016 Presidential Election that it was effectively declaring itself a sanctuary state in which California taxpayers would foot the bill to provide legal defense and protection for illegal immigrants within its borders threatened with deportation by the US Government in accordance with US law.

Likewise in New York, how can the millions of regular conservative and Republican voters continue to live such as those upstate and in the Finger lakes region, and by implication, support with their tax dollars the likes of Hillary Clinton, Chuck Schumer, Eliot Spitzer, David Paterson, and Democratic Governor Cuomo? It was current Democratic NY Governor Cuomo who said that conservatives had no place in NY State. I in turn say to such conservatives what stronger invitation does one need to leave? Why stay where one is clearly not wanted? Also, what about those many conservative and Republican voters in Illinois-still called the "Land of Lincoln," such as those in downstate Illinois, who today are forced to support via their tax dollars the likes of the Chicago Daley machine, former Illinois Governor Blago, and of course until recently, former US Senator Barack Hussein Obama?

How can conservatives in these respective states-and there are many, though unfortunately, they do not constitute a majority-continue to live in these states and by implication support their leftist Democratic state governments and elected officials who surely do not represent them, and certainly not their conservative values? Indeed, the many thousands of linchpin, taxpaying and voting conservative and Republican residents of the states of California, New York, New Jersey, and Illinois-as well as those conservatives who reside in the other smaller states which regularly vote for the Democratic candidate in national election years: i.e.. states such as Vermont, Oregon, Hawaii, etc.-constitute among the most productive residents of their states, and this is no less true than those who unfortunately reside in all the of the country's most left-leaning states today.

Most conservatives-even those who reside in say, New York or California-regularly pay their taxes; obey the law; take care of their families; and fulfill their obligation to their God. By their very nature in the way that they live their lives, conservatives in this country-even in the most left-leaning of states-provide an order and structure which is essential to the societies in which they reside. As of this writing, the country as a whole-as well as many of the individual states-particularly many of the left-leaning states such as California, New York, Pennsylvania, etc.-all of which supported Obama in the 2008 Presidential Election-are in very dire economic straits. How much more desperate would say the economic condition of such high-tax, left-leaning states as California and New York be without the stability provided to them by their conservative residents who work their jobs and businesses; pay their taxes; and continue to maintain their ordered and law-abiding existences without fall?

It is time for conservatives in California and New York in particular, but also in the certain other perennially left-leaning Democratic states to re-examine why they continue to live and pay their taxes where they do? Why do they consent to live as virtual slaves in states in which the state governments are unresponsive to them at best, and condescending if not hostile to them at worst? Conservatives in California and New York by their continuing to live in these states contribute to the continued propping up of a flawed and oppressive political system of excessive taxes, and socialist and secular-progressive ideology. This nation fought and won a war in 1776 over the issue of taxation without representation. It can hardly be argued that in the manner in which they exist today, that the interests of conservatives are represented by their present state governments of California and New York, plus the several other traditionally left-leaning states as well.

Yet conservatives do possess and maintain-and should utilize-the freedom, which is their birthright, secures by our Fathers in 1776, and refreshed by American blood spilled in all of our wars fought since then. If the socialistic and left-wing state governments in California and New York, plus other the states does little more for the loyal conservative residents of their states other than suck them dry of ever-increasing tax revenue to fund their ever-increasing socialistic schemes, conservatives can and should strike the chains of socialistic bondage from their ankles. Conservatives do not-and should not-any longer prop up with their hard-earned tax dollars state governments run by liberal/left Democrats who do not represent their individual interests, and indeed frequently mock them and view conservatives as only a reliable funding source. Instead, conservatives should move! They have the absolute freedom to do so as American citizens and indeed given the perilous state of the country today due to the political strength of the liberal left and the Obama Presidency, I state that true conservatives who can move-and admittedly not all can, though many can-should move!

I state without reservation the dedicated loyal American conservatives have no business residing in the states of California, and New York in particular, in the present state of affairs. They are badly outnumbered in these states and can contribute nothing constructive politically to the improvement and salvation of this nation by remaining where they are and are regularly voting-even for lost causes. For the conservative movement in America today to wield its maximum political impact, conservatives must consolidate, and maximize their number and political strength in politically and ideology-friendly states (i.e.. clear Republican, or Republican-leaning).

Also, conservatives can gravitate towards those states where conservatives and Republicans have achieved and maintained a rough parity with the Democrats and the leftists: i.e.. states such as Pennsylvania. However as already noted, states such as California, New York, New Jersey, and Illinois-among others-where there are significant numbers of conservative and Republican voters residing-but who are nonetheless outnumbered by the leftists and the Democrats-is a luxury in which the best interests of the conservatives themselves-plus that of the nation-can no longer again afford. The chess match in which we are engaged at present with the Democratic left for the control and direction of this nation via the Electoral College is not one in which we are at present winning. However, it will begin to turn in conservative's favor once conservatives stop assisting their political adversaries on the left by inflating the Electoral Vote totals (plus again assisting the economic stability and strength) of those large states where the Democratic left now controls by continuing to live-and vote- there (i.e.. again, California and New York).

If a process begins by which the Democratic vote strength and Electoral College totals ebbs from the combination of say the states of California, New York, New Jersey, and Illinois with a corresponding increase in Republican and conservative popular and Electoral College votes from other states, this nation may yet be saved from both the Democratic left and socialism. This process to save the nation from both the Democratic left and socialism is entirely in control of the American conservatives themselves. By the movement towards a Red State Nation and the marshalling of their tremendous political power, American conservatives whose love of this country is boundless can work together in common purpose for the preservation of this nation, our Judeo-Christian heritage, and our free enterprise economy from the socialists, and secular-progressives. In the march towards a Red State Nation in order to conserve this nation, its institutions and heritage in its present form, conservatives will truly be fulfilling their lives' mission that they were meant to do.

In the continuing chess match with the Democratic left for the permanent political control of this country via the Electoral College, American conservatives are somewhat fortunate. This is in that only a few large perennially-voting Democratic states require conservative attrition in order to significantly alter the American political landscape. Conservative population migration from just the four usual-Democratic states that have at length already been discussed: California, New York, Illinois, and New Jersey would reap great benefits for the conservative cause in the attempt to gain political control of the country. Again, the intent is two-fold: to reduce the population of large population states that in normal election years vote for the Democratic Presidential candidate; and to correspondingly increase the conservative and Republican votes in neighboring Republican-leaning or even swing states.

If this trend is started-and maintained-of conservative and Republican out-migration from the large Democratic states to Republican-leaning and swing states, eventually a permanent and positive shift will occur in the Electoral College to the benefit of conservatives as the states of California, New York, Illinois, and New Jersey all continue to lose population-and votes in the Electoral College-to more Republican-friendly states. Conservative out-migration from California-particularly Southern California and Orange County-to nearby states such as Arizona, Nevada, Colorado, New Mexico, etc. will greatly augment the already-considerable Republican strength in those states while it will correspondingly weaken Democratic-voting California in the Electoral College due to the population loss.

Likewise conservative out-migration from Illinois-especially downstate-to any or all of Illinois' neighboring states: Kentucky,

Missouri, Iowa, Wisconsin, Indiana, etc.-plus also to states slightly further away such as Tennessee and Arkansas-will in turn greatly increase the Republican electoral strength in any of those states at the expense of the Democratic strength in Illinois. Conservative out-migration from both New York and New Jersey would be similar in that both states in and of themselves are neighbor states, and also it could have considerable impact in that both states have a significant conservative and Republican base population (in New York, in the upstate, particularly the far upstate and Finger Lakes regions while in New Jersey, particularly in South Jersey).

One critical beneficiary of conservative out-migration from both New York and New Jersey would be neighboring (for both) Pennsylvania, traditionally classified as a swing state, but in more recent national elections has been trending increasingly Democratic. The infusion of thousands of additional Republican and conservative-minded voters into Pennsylvania from both New York and New Jersey where such voters have but modest impact in a national election, could instead have very significant consequences in a national election.

In the last several national elections: particularly 2000, 2004, 2008, 2012, and 2016-Pennsylvania was a true battleground state and was most vigorously contested between the Democratic and Republican Presidential candidates, although in all three races the Democratic candidate won (in 2004, only by 2% though). One of the frequently-cited caveats in American national Presidential elections is that the Democratic candidate cannot win unless his (or her) collection of states includes Pennsylvania. This was proven in 2016 when GOP candidate Donald Trump did narrowly carry Pennsylvania, depriving it-and ultimately the White House-from Democratic candidate Hillary Clinton. If so, it is obvious that if Pennsylvania was already a battleground state in national elections, the infusion of thousands of additional conservatives and Republican voters from both New York and New Jersey will certainly make it even more so.

In addition to Pennsylvania, conservative and Republican voters from New York and New Jersey could migrate to Virginia, North Carolina, and also Florida where they could lend a most significant impact to existing Republican electoral strength in these states, especially since all three were won by Democrat, Obama in 2008 after previous been won by Republican, Bush in 2000 and 2004. In addition, Republican voters in Western New York could migrate to Ohio to augment already-considerable Republican strength there.

The exodus of thousands of tax-paying, responsible, and employed conservative citizens from heretofore irresponsible, Democratic, and ill-managed states such as New York, California, and Illinois could be just the strong medicine that these states, their government officials, and the remaining and predominantly-Democratic residents may need to wake up and to see the errors of their ways. Yes, this can be just the first step to transform even states such as California, New York, and Illinois into "Red" states themselves. To let these irresponsible, high-tax, reckless spending, and far-left social engineering states deal with the consequences of their many years of poor fiscal and social governance, coupled with the major erosion of their own tax base which the out-migration of large numbers of their productive conservative citizens to more hospitable states would result in-and would be very strong- appropriate-medicine (cold turkey, etc.)

Forcing financially and socially irresponsible left-wing states such as California and New York in particular to reform themselves while perhaps thousands of their most productive and responsible conservative citizens and neighbors are moving out of them could indeed be the strong kick necessary to force them to reform themselves which these states need, plus as the initial step to eventually transform themselves into Red states as well.

Another advantage to the conservatives who migrate from the large, Democratic high-tax states is that in nearly every conceivable instance, they would be moving to another state where they would pay less in state taxes than they would in the state that they would be leaving behind. Particularly California, New York, and New Jersey-all very high tax states-movement from any one of these three to any of the states surrounding them-particularly in the case of moving from New York or New Jersey to Pennsylvania -would result in significant tax savings for the expense and inconvenience of essentially moving next door.

As now seen, conservative exodus in large numbers from otherwise large Democratic majority states can have a very profound impact on the Electoral College in the ongoing chess match between the left and the right in the political control of this country. Yes, conservatives by their decisions to move from large Democrat states where not only does their votes essentially not count, but their continued residence-and continued political participation-in one of these states helps their leftist adversaries in that it keeps the Electoral Vote total of these states unnecessarily inflated in the Democrats favor. And in addition, as already shown, permits these rogue, virtually criminal LW states from dealing with the consequences of their badly misguided policies.

In addition to encouraging Republican and conservatives to migrate to Republican-friendly states in order to maximize Republican electoral strength, an additional incentive for the migration would be for the Republican-friendly states themselves to initiate and maintain programs to encourage Republican and conservative immigration into their states. South Carolina several years ago initiated and advertised a program to encourage conservative-minded residents from other states to migrate there, and certainly other Red States can do the same. No state currently has-or would suffer from-an over-abundance of productive, tax-paying, God-fearing, new conservative residents, and voters. Republican-minded states can compete for the conservatives migrating from the leftist states just the same as they now compete for relocating businesses and industries. Republican states can offer to these seeking-to-relocate conservatives such incentives and aids such as tax incentives, relocation assistance, informational websites, etc.

It is to the mutual advantage of current Republican states such as South Carolina, Alabama, and Oklahoma-plus their current residents-to reach out, encourage, and offer welcome-to the many thousands of present conservatives and Republicans who currently reside in such states as California, New York, Illinois, and New Jersey-and who might otherwise consider moving to a more hospitable environment, or perhaps already is considering to. The joining together of conservatives across this country in conservative and Republican-friendly states in order to maximize their tremendous political power, profits all: the Republican-friendly states; their current residents; the conservative emigrants from the Democratic states, and of course, the nation.

If conservatives nationwide can seize the mantle and if the movement towards a Red State Nation begins with conservatives and Republicans starting to emigrate from the Democratic states to the Republican ones, it is a movement that could be-and should be-centrally coordinated, and central coordination could be useful for many reasons. It could provide an interface between the conservatives in the Democrat states seeking to move or considering to do so, and the various Republican states to which they would eventually move to. A central coordination or management office of the Red State Nation effort could provide an educational, informational, and a motivational impetus to the overall effort by reaching out to the conservatives in the Democrat states and providing to them the information, assistance, and encouragement to join the effort. Perhaps at least at the outset of a Red State Nation effort, a central coordination function could be launched and managed in conjunction with the Tea Party movement, or with assistance by the Tea Party.

Likewise, a central coordination or management office for the Red State Nation effort could provide invaluable assistance to the overall effort in the host Republican states themselves. Targeted towards conservatives in the Democrat states, websites could be created and advertising generated highlighting low tax rates, new housing developments, attractive homesites, retirement communities, employment opportunities, recreational venues, (i.e.. parks, beaches, lakes, mountain resorts, etc.) in the Republican states. As an interface with the conservative émigrés in the Democrat states, the central coordination or management function of the Red State Nation effort could effectively communicate at the state-wide level in the Republican states the need for adoption of émigré-friendly policies to both attract, and to assist in the transition for the conservative émigrés from the Democrat states.

The central coordination function might eventually be able to assist in and possibly, ultimately direct the flow of the conservative émigrés to specific targeted Republican states such as Virginia, North Carolina, Florida, Colorado, Nevada, etc. in order to enhance Republican election efforts in the Electoral College. The Obama years in particular have been hard on North Carolina, and especially Virginia. Many illegal immigrants, Muslim refugees, and immigrants have been routed to both states to increase their Democratic voter registration. Far Northern Virginia in the Washington D.C. suburbs have greatly increased in Democratic voter registration due to the great increase in unionized Federal Government workers during the eight Obama years. The GOP must reclaim Virginia as a consistently voting red state once again (it has not voted GOP since the 2004 Presidential Election). Also, the GOP must reinforce and strengthen North Carolina which though not as far gone as Virginia is, is nonetheless very near the tipping point. It is also conceivable that the central coordination function might actually develop to where say through volunteer efforts it can both stimulate and assist the amount of conservative emigration from the Democrat states by offering to the émigrés actual movement assistance; assisting in the packing of émigrés' household belongings; and even assistance (volunteer trucks, etc..) in the actual movement of the émigré households to their new homes in the Republican states.

The movement of many thousands of Republican and conservatives from their present homes in traditional Democrat states is not a small endeavor, nor without its complications; however, it is a vital and necessary one in the effort to preserve this nation and its future from the very real threat of socialism now presently before us. For those millions of conservatives in this land whose love of this nation in peril burns like an unquenchable fire within, it is a task that is neither too difficult nor unnecessary.

As already mentioned, the concentration of the Red State Nation's primary emphasis on stimulating Republican and conservative emigration from specific Democratic states should be placed on four specific states: California, New York, Illinois, and New Jersey. These are large population states with many thousands of Republican and conservative voters though again in most elections-particular in national ones-not enough Republican and conservative voters to carry the state. Therefore, the greatest potential return in the number of conservative émigrés to move to Republican-friendly states would come from these four states, at least from the outset.

However, there are a number of other states which regularly vote Democratic also. Republican and conservative emigration from these states should nonetheless be encouraged also, even though the Republican and conservative base votes and potential émigrés in these other states are much smaller than that that which currently exists in the other-and larger-four. These other and regular Democratic states would include such states as: Maine, Vermont, Massachusetts, Connecticut, Delaware, Maryland, Washington, and Oregon. In each instance in these states, conservatives and Republicans would not have to relocate far as they could easily emigrate to a neighboring Republican or tossup state. All of these states voted for the Democratic presidential candidate in 2008, 2012, and 2016.

Emigres from the states of Maine, Vermont, Massachusetts, and Connecticut could easily move to next-door New Hampshire, as well-a balanced tossup state. Likewise, émigrés from Delaware and Maryland could easily move to their neighbor Virginia which they share the Delmarva Peninsula with, and which until most recently was considered a traditional Republican and conservative state.-at least until Barack Obama won the Old Dominion state in the 2008 Presidential

Election. Also, Republicans and conservatives who presently reside in the states of Washington and Oregon could easily move to next-door Idaho, a bell-weather Republican and conservative state. Even the emigration of thousands of Republicans and conservatives from the state of Minnesota to say the nominally "Red" states of North and South Dakota would be helpful to help send packing Democratic US Senators which nonetheless managed to get themselves elected in both of these nominal Red states as of 2009. The Republican Party is competitive in Minnesota and did recently have a respected Republican Governor in Tim Pawlenty. In the 2016 Presidential Election, President Trump and Vice President Pence campaigned extensively in Minnesota and ultimately lost the state by less than 2%.

However, the Republican Party in Minnesota could not protect the US Senate seat of Republican Norm Coleman in the 2008 election from being snatched by far-left Democrat radical Al Franken following a highly-disputed and dubious election recount process, and after Franken had been behind on election night. It is perhaps only fitting that Minnesota conservative émigrés would assist in turning out Democratic senators in North and South Dakota after having been unable to protect one of their own in Minnesota. One of the highlights of this recount process was boxes of votes being found in the trunk of a Minnesota Democratic election worker's car, which of course were ultimately counted.

In each instance, such developments-if successful-would have a profound impact on the balance of power in the Electoral College in favor of the Republicans, subtracting collective strength from the listed grouping of Democrat states while enhancing Republican strength in the already-Republican favorable states of New Hampshire, Virginia, North Dakota, South Dakota, and Idaho.

In addition to the reasons already displayed, a Red State Nation strategy adopted by the conservatives and the Republican Party in this country would be an effective counter to the Democratic strategy of utilizing ACORN, the outfit utilized by the Democrats to supposedly register new voters, but is instead mired in vote fraud allegations in just about every state they have operated in. Rather than the fraudulent practices of the Democratic Left and the ACORN operatives of fraudulently "registering" what frequently amounts to mythical "new" voters in various states, there is nothing at all even remotely fraudulent about the Red State Nation project outlined here. Red State Nation again involves the actual the actual movement of actual Republican and conservative voters from usual-Democratic voting states to either specified tossup states, Republican-leaning states, or strong-Republican states.

Indeed, as witnessed by the Democratic and ACORN machinations with voting totals and fraudulent new voter registrations, plus voting by dead people, illegal aliens, foreign immigrants, etc. in various critical states such as Ohio, Nevada, Missouri in the 2008 Presidential Election, plus the elections since with the fraudulent ACORN component now apparently permanently added to the Democratic arsenal as a tool to win national elections, Red State Nation as a counter-veiling conservative and Republican strategy takes an even greater significance. If the Democrats in national Presidential elections are going to continue to contest the Republicans in critical swing states such as say, Ohio, with what amounts to almost organized, institutionalized fraud which is what ACORN amounts to, Republicans and conservatives can no longer afford to allow millions of their legitimate voters languish in Democratic-majority states such as California, Illinois, New York, and New Jersey where they would have but minimal impact on the election. Rather they should attempt to relocate these voters to other states where they would have a much greater impact on the Electoral College. It is simply a matter of re-positioning chess pieces on the chess board as the Jeff Goldblum character in the movie, "Independence Day" would heartily agree

The Democratic left by utilizing fraud to win elections via groups like ACORN demonstrate their firm resolve to win at all costs regardless of the method and ethical deficiencies involved. Republicans and conservatives can likewise leave no stone unturned-or trump card played, such as Red State Nation- in order to counter the left and to win as well. The future of this nation is at stake here. The one contrast in which we will not compete with the left however is that one for the for the most ethical deficiencies. We must-and shall-allow the Democratic left win that title by default. We conservatives must attempt to win again-and lead-but only by competing-and leading-via ethical standards which are beyond reproach. We do not need to attempt to steal elections via fraudulent ACORN-type groups and methods in order to win. There are still enough good people in this country who will follow us, and vote for us when we properly run and lead while building towards our Red State Nation.

CHAPTER 3:

To Build a Red State Nation.

It is true that particularly in the very challenging and difficult economic times under the Obama Presidency, conservatives, even those of means, could not just get up and move to another state. Houses have to be sold; Jobs have to be quit, found, or relocated, etc. It would be a somewhat easier experience for retired or semi-retired conservatives to move from their present homes in the designated Democrat states where there would be minimal impact upon present employment. In many instances as already discussed movement from their present homes in Democrat states would be to the financial advantage to the conservative retirees. In nearly all instances they would be moving from a higher tax situation in their present state to a lower tax situation in their new Republican state. Also, self-employed, or entrepreneurial conservatives could perhaps with only modest difficulty relocate to another state and in short order restart their business pursuit from their previous location. In many instances, conservatives relocating to a "Red" or Republican state could move to a state such as Florida or Texas where they would pay no state income tax at all.

In addition, other savings may be realized such as lower energy costs as well as in moving from such cold Northern states such as Illinois, New York, New Jersey, plus those in New England to warmer or more temperate states further south. In any event, any movement however small at first towards the formation of the "Red State Nation" will be a positive development for the country. In life, most change or new developments start with the taking of "baby steps." All conservatives who now can-and will start to take the baby steps-towards the transformation of this nation to a Red State Nation-may just be enough to draw this nation back from the brink of socialism. Hopefully in time, the baby steps today will soon become a toddlers leaning into a brisk walk and ultimately a sprint as all conservatives rise un and join the movement to transform this nation into a Red State Nation.

As previously noted, the nationwide movement of both Republicans and conservatives from traditional Democratic-voting states to usual-Republican-voting states-as well as swing states-will accomplish much and will help in the formation of a Red State Nation, but by itself will not be enough. As cited previously, for the Republican Party to regain and hold national political leadership, it must retain a consistent 40% of the Hispanic vote. And again, this task, while not an easy one, is certainly attainable. With eventual illegal immigration reform, a certainty in some form either sooner or later, it is imperative that the Republican Party does not surrender to the Democrats altogether, the image and symbol of the party that is sympathetic to the hopes and aspirations of Hispanics for a better life in this nation. Should the Republicans do this then permanent two class political status to the Democrats in this country is very nearly assured, regardless of how many white conservatives they may successfully encourage to move out of nominal Democratic-voting states. The continued Democratic emphasis on population expansion-and voter participation-via continued illegal immigration is a threat to jobs as well as wage growth, and thereby should assist the GOP in continuing to expand its' outreach and support among African-Americans as well.

There is every reason to hope that the initiation of a bone-fide partnership between the ascending Hispanic minority in this country, and the Republican Party with their conservative allies is a natural outgrowth of their many shared principles of pro-family, pro-religion, pro-traditional marriage, pro-work and entrepreneurship, pro-country, and anti-socialism. Abandoning the Hispanic community altogether to the Democratic left where it doesn't naturally fit-even given the emotionalism surrounding the illegal immigration issue-would virtually be criminal negligence by the Republican Party as well as virtual suicide. Again, the Republican Party remaining as a virtual white man's enclave in 21st Century America is an entity doomed to defeat, and probable eventual extinction.

Conservative principles which find their natural home in the Republican Party are timeless, and with broad political appeal. It is our duty and obligation as conservatives to proselytize our principles and their benefit to make them-and our movement and the Republican Party-as exposed, known, and as open to as many people as possible. Our task is not unlike that of the Disciples of Christ whose task was to spread the Gospel, or even that of the original patriots in the earliest days of the Republic who were charged to proclaim liberty throughout the land. As were Christ's Disciples and our nation's earliest patriots, we can be no less vigilant to spread the word as our nation's very future is at stake.

If the Republican Party and their conservative allies begin to reach out and embrace the concerns of the Hispanic community and continue to welcome the fellowship of their conservative Hispanic brethren, plus begin, and accelerate the process of conservative emigration from the Democratic-left states, a national reaction will be the Electoral College results in subsequent national elections. Tea Party members can be anticipated to be among the most enthusiastic of the émigrés from the Blue States though by no means should they be anticipated to be all or nearly all of the total number of émigrés.

I visualize a national restructuring of the national restructuring of the Electoral College map essentially along the lines of the Bush reelection effort of 2004 with the possible exception of New Mexico being a Red Republican State rather than a Blue Democratic State with all else being equal other than the states of Pennsylvania and New Hampshire might hopefully be other states that would flip to "Red, " as indeed Pennsylvania finally did flip in 2016, and New Hampshire very nearly did. If the process would continue whereby conservative American Hispanics, Republicans, and conservatives would continue to participate and migrate from those Democratic/left states where they have no voice to Red States, the salvation of the United States from socialism will be greatly assured. Conservatives would then no longer have to wring their hands over the current seemingly hopeless position of the country as they can unite to continue and further this process to its fruition just as they have done to advance the interests of the national Tea Party effort to its great participatory success. Now conservatives can unite to facilitate lasting change by simply moving and/or assisting other patriots to move in order to facilitate our Red State Nation.

The creation of a Red State Nation of nominally voting Republican states of sufficient number in national elections to control the majority of the Electoral College, does create an opposite effect which does give room for pause when considering he political health of the country. That is that in establishing as a sort of "line of demarcation" where the Red States of the "Red State Nation" begin, you are at the same time establishing a line where the Blue States (Democrat) end. The near-permanent freezing of dividing lines between the country's "Red" States and "Blue" States creates the possibility of also freezing into place a divided country, and intense political conflict across definitive boundaries. It is hard however to fathom at the time of this writing in 2016 how the United States can possibly be more divided and conflicted than it is now-possibly as divided-if not more so-than in the years immediately before the Civil War.

This possibility brings to mind and American "Iron Curtain" such as existed in 1950's Europe separating the free democratic European nations from those contained within the then Eastern European Communist bloc. Even more relevant-and perhaps disturbing-a dividing line establishing a Red State Nation line of states brings to mind the pre-Civil War 19* Century Missouri Compromise line which separated the free and slave states. The net effect of the implementation of a Red State Nation effort resulting in the gradual removal of conservative and traditional Republican voters from Blue and dark-Blue states into legitimate "Red" states and "tossup" states in order to flip them "Red" would essentially result in a modern-day recreation of the Missouri Compromise line which rather than dividing the country to the Pacific Ocean separating free states from slave, would instead separate Red states from Blue, Republican from Democrat. Freezing unofficial boundary lines into place through the heart of a divided nation which separate opposing states and principles of government is cause for some concern.

Again, I stress "unofficial" boundary lines. I certainly do not advocate any legal restrictions (even if they would be remotely Constitutional when they clearly would not be) which would prohibit or restrict conservatives from residing in say, Vermont or New York, or liberals or leftists from residing in Tennessee or Alabama. This is unlike restrictions which existed prior to the Civil War then pertaining to the ownership of slaves depending upon what state you resided in either north or south of the Missouri Compromise line. Indeed, following the ideal Red State Nation model which I have been attempting to construct here, I could visualize the new and again, "unofficial," "Mason-Dixon Line" separating Red states from Blue one state north from where it presently exists moving it to the New York-Pennsylvania border from its' present Maryland-Pennsylvania border.

However again, the purpose for the establishment of Red State nation in the first place is the establishment of a political coalition which will insure the triumph of conservative and Republican candidates every four years by the majority control of the Electoral College. Once Republican control is established and the nation is rescued from high taxation and socialism, the state of political conflict can perhaps transform from the establishment of Red State Nation and political control of the country to the transformation of the nation itself via the attempt to gain political control of the individual Blue

(Democrat) states. This second or transformational process to convert current "Blue" or Democrat states into regularly voting "Red" or Republican states is certainly not anticipated to be brief or easy and is a subject for a follow-up effort.

The grave fiscal crisis in California in 2009 with the Golden State looking at a multi-billion-dollar shortfall and near -certain large tax increases is for one, already causing many residents and businesses to flee to neighboring states. The Red State Nation project would simply accelerate the process in California which had already begun by California's own mismanagement and spendthrift ways. Texas has greatly benefited from emigration from California, according to former Texas Governor Rick Perry. The State of New York with its already high level of tax burden-plus the prospect of more to come-is probably not far behind California and is ripe also for a Red State Nation project. With many of New York's residents easily able to relocate to neighboring PA whose relative level of taxation (outside of the City of Philadelphia) remains far lower than that of New York, a flood of Republican and conservative émigrés fleeing New York for the more tax-friendly confines of Pennsylvania would both benefit the émigrés themselves, and the nation. The benefit to the nation from this process would be that Pennsylvania is already a near swing state in national elections; with PA inundated with New York émigrés fleeing high New York taxes, this could easily tip Pennsylvania over into a "Red" or Republican state and thus greatly harming the Democrats' ability to win national elections. The Democratic Presidential candidate has won every election in Pennsylvania since 1992, until again GOP Donald Trump won it in 2016.

The Red State Nation project would also be a benefit to the nation in that it would serve to greatly unify the nation. In stimulating a mass exodus of conservative and Republican émigrés from what is now chiefly Northern states such as New York, New Jersey, and Illinois, etc. into Southern states, the intermix of Northern and Southern natives within the same states as fellow conservatives and Republican citizens could not help but to have a unifying effect. It would then serve to dampen the kind of pro-secession talk that was recently associated with the state of Texas and the Texas Governor, Rick Perry. Red State Nation's designed immigration of Northern state Republicans and conservatives-as well as those from other parts of the country-into the Southern "Red" states in particular would greatly serve to reassure the conservative residents of the Southern states that they are not alone or isolated as conservative citizens of this country; that they are valuable, respected, and necessary elements both of the broad conservative movement of the country, as well as the linchpin of the reclamation and salvation of the nation itself. Red State Nation would not succeed without the willing and enthusiastic assistance and participation of the conservative citizens of the Southern (and other) Red states. This enthusiastic assistance and participation in the Red State Nation effort by the present Southern as well as the conservative citizens of other Red states (I am sure) will never flag.

The relocation of Northern and Democratic state conservatives into pre-existing "Red" or Republican states will not only increase the Republican states population, Congressional-and Electoral College-representation -and with a corresponding decrease of all of these factors in the "Blue" or Democrat states from which they are leaving , but also their emigration should serve to make the "Red" states into which they are entering more conservative or right-leaning with an even larger conservative population contained in the individual "Red" states. This process once begun should result in conservative Republican representatives serving in the US Congress that are more conservative than before; reflective of the demographics change going on within their districts, plus a greater quantity of them which is reflective of the conservative population influx. This is the genesis of Red State Nation. This increase of the number of American conservatives into our existing Red states-this greater concentration-will not only serve to make our existing Red states more "Red," but will also serve to make the nation as a whole, more "Red" as well.

CHAPTER 4:

SHALL WE OVERCOME? COMPLICATIONS TO A RED STATE NATION.

An additional impetus for the need for the growth of the idea of a Red State Nation is the tax and socialistic designs of the Obama Administration itself; particularly against the nation's wealthiest taxpayers-especially in the (already) high-tax states of California and New York. With the implementation of the Obama Administration's Cap and Trade Energy policies, plus nationalized health care programs (Obamacare), high-end tax payers in both New York and California were looking at combined federal-state income tax percentage of over 50%. In addition, high-end taxpayers residing in New York City with its additional local tax levies were looking at a collective tax percentage of over 60%! This is true confiscatory socialism at its worst. What additional incentive is needed for these taxpayers to seriously consider to move to a lower tax state-in some instances-states with no state income tax whatsoever? Why would not these taxpayers seriously consider moving from the source of these oppressive taxes, as inconvenient as it may be? And, regardless of how many of these high-end taxpayers may have voted in the past; how could they as hard-working and productive people watch so much of their wealth taken and in many instances mis-used and just wasted by their government to finance various socialistic schemes?

And how can these former high-end income-and Democratic voters-realize the error of their previous political thinking and become enthusiastic citizens and advocates for the Red State Nation?

Hopefully for many of them it does-and will become easy or easier- to realize the mistakes of their previous political voting when they would relocate to a more conservative and Republican voting state where the tax rates are significantly lower than in California and New York-again in some instances where there are no state income taxes at all.

On the other hand, as already documented by the continuing voting patterns of many Democratic voters throughout the country, it is indeed difficult for many of this particular breed of cat to change their stripes, regardless of how compelling it may seem that the argument is that they should do so. As already noted, in many of our major metropolitan centers within the last several years-and in some instances, it is a process which has spanned decades-many of the former residents of the inner cities moved to the outlying suburbs surrounding the cities. These residents fled their former homes in the cities to escape crime, ever-escalating taxes; deteriorating city services-particularly schools, and a declining quality of life.

As most of these cities have experienced decades of one-party left-wing Democratic rule only, the declining quality of life and declining attractiveness in residency in these cities is chiefly tied to their legacy of this one-party, Democratic rule. However, many of their former residents who have moved out, were and have remained Democrats themselves, and have inexplicably continued their previous, pro-Democratic voting patterns in their new homes. One would think that former inner-city residents who have experienced first-hand, the poor results of living under one-party, left-wing Democratic rule and also were successful in escaping from it, would be the wiser for the experience and would leave their individual Democratic legacies behind them along with their former homes at the city line when they moved out. Sadly, in all too many instances that has not been the case.

Take the example of Philadelphia, PA. again, along with the great demographic impact that the out-migration of Philadelphia residents has had on particularly the political landscape for both the Republican and Democratic parties in national elections in Pennsylvania. Decades ago, the four suburban counties surrounding Philadelphia: Bucks, Montgomery, Chester, and Delaware were predominantly Republican and provided a great counterweight in national election years to the overwhelming Democratic majorities reported out of Philadelphia. Today that is no longer the case as in recent national elections the Philadelphia suburban counties have started to report Democratic majorities themselves to supplement the large ones-though reduced-still originating out of Philadelphia. It is no accident therefore that Pennsylvania has voted the Democratic candidate in every Presidential election since 1992-the last five to be specific, although again in 2016, Pennsylvania did flip to GOP candidate, Donald Trump.

The reason for the voting trend change in the Philadelphia, PA suburbs in the last few decades is simple: the attrition rate of former Democratic-voting Philadelphia residents (many thousands) who fled the City with its' myriad problems during these years to the safer environs of the Philadelphia suburbs, and who continued their Democratic-voting ways once they had resettled there. Why former Philadelphia residents fled the City of Philadelphia, PA with its one-party Democratic rule and its myriad urban problems directly resulting from that one-party rule, only to continue their Democratic-voting ways in their new suburban homes seems to defy logic-except presumably to leftists and other Democratic-inclined voters. Spreading LW cancer seemingly makes no one the wiser, it seems.

Former Republican US Senator from Pennsylvania-and a well-known conservative spokesman-Rick Santorum, lost his bid for re-election in the 2006 election in the wake of the anti-Bush, anti-Iraq near feverous sentiment which particularly gripped Pennsylvania that year. As of this writing, he was recently heard to quip on a Fox News telecast that "Eastern Pennsylvania should be given to New Jersey," referring to Philadelphia, its suburban environs, and the various east, central and north-eastern cities of Allentown, Bethlehem, Easton, Wilkes-Barre, and Scranton. Santorum of course, hails from Western Pennsylvania, and within Pennsylvania there is a great rivalry between the eastern and western portions of the state, fueled in no small measure by both the political and sports rivalry between Pennsylvania's two largest cities: Philadelphia (eastern), and Pittsburg (western).

Santorum's quip, understandable by virtue of his clear Western Pennsylvania bias, is nonetheless a bit extreme. Yes, Eastern Pennsylvania from Philadelphia and its suburbs extending northwards do collectively comprise of perhaps the most consistently Democratic voting areas in the state. And Eastern Pennsylvania can be-and frequently is-viewed as an extension of (Dark-Blue) Democrat New Jersey, while Western Pennsylvania is frequently viewed as an extension of normally Republican-voting West Virginia and Ohio. Also as already touched on, the City of Philadelphia with its hard-left politics, numerous and militant unions, aggressive minorities who now collectively comprise a majority of the City's declining population; and last (but not least), its well-known reputation for pro-Democratic voting fraud-perhaps surpassed only by Obama's Chicago-obviously presents a unique set of challenges to overcome in order to remake Pennsylvania as a consistently-voting "Red" state. However yes, it can be done, and as provided by the results of the 2016 Presidential Election, hopefully now-consistently so.

As the socialist agenda of Barack Hussein Obama and his leftist Democratic allies in 2009 had continued to gather steam in Washington with their massive spending schemes; increased taxes; anti-white bigotry from the appointment of leftist judges to the Federal judiciary; Bermuda vacations for terrorists exiles from the Guantanamo Bay detention center; taxpayer bank rolling of ACORN to continue their election fraud activities; and sweetheart bankruptcy plans for automakers GM and Chrysler which primarily benefit union allies at the UAW rather than legitimate primary creditors; opposition to these actions by determined, yet outnumbered and outgunned Republicans in and out of Congress, was spirited, yet futile. The brazen character of the Obama agenda has clearly upset, angered, and made nervous many productive, affluent, conservative and Republican Americans-including conservative commentator, Rush Limbaugh-and whispering by many of buying land for moving overseas has grown louder. Some have publicly-others quietly-either investigated-or actively pursued-the prospects of either moving-or at least property ownership in other countries.

The concentration though through intra-state emigration which Red State Nation represents in the effort to prevent socialism in America can truly forestall a much greater calamity in the permanent removal of American wealth, expertise, and influential leadership to other countries. If a mass exodus to other countries of American conservatives and Republicans would begin to commence the only effective check to the excesses of the Democratic left would be removed, and America's current march towards socialism would be greatly accelerated.

An advent of a Red State Nation effort of the movement of conservatives from heretofore primarily Democratic voting states to Red or Republican states, it is to be expected that there would be objections, perhaps even likely strong ones from the Republican Party, organizations, or Republican officials from it-in the source Democratic state being vacated. It might frequently be determined that the most complaining of a Red State Nation effort in these states would be from so-called RINO's (Republicans In Name Only), and not in most instances from true conservative Republicans.

Given that the Red State Nation effort would necessarily be a national one to save the nation from far-left Democratic socialism, such protests, and objections, while given polite deference, should not be taken too-strongly. As of this writing, the New York State Congressional delegation includes just 3 Republicans, as opposed to nearly 30 Democrats with of course both New York US Senators being Democratic. If the Republican Parties in the states of California, New York, and Illinois in particular had been doing their jobs and kept their states competitive with the Democrats in most local, state, and in particular, national elections, there would be no need for a Red State Nation project to save the nation from far-left Democratic socialism. What Republican office holders there are in these Democrat-majority states-again, more than likely being RINO's-are such because they frequently must temper what pro-conservative/pro-Republican viewpoints that they may have in order for political survival in their states in order to attract sufficient Democratic voters necessary to win elections.

The goal of the Red State Nation in maintaining national conservative Republican political power in specific conservative/Republican majority states is to create a conservative political environment in which Republicans no longer have to seek votes from Democrats in order to achieve political power. In such an environment, Republican candidates need not compromise their true conservative political principles and instincts, and also in such a political environment, the most conservative candidate can succeed and truly flourish, i.e.. The cream can literally rise to the top.

In the Electoral College, the national Democratic Party has built a nearly-impregnable position of Electoral Votes in the block consisting of the votes from California, Illinois, and New York which again gives the Democrats a most unfair advantage-and significant portion-towards the winning total of 270. Regardless of the sensibilities of Republican Party officials and office holders in individual states, Republicans and conservatives need to do whatever they can to deny victory to the Democrats and to save the nation from far-left Democratic socialism. Red State Nation as a program of action is designed to do just that.

Despite the election to the Presidency of Barack Hussein Obama, the United States according to consistent polls remains predominantly a center/right nation. Obama's election in 2008, I would describe as an "accident of history." It was an accident in that the leftist Democratic Party nominated an extremist for President; an extremist with both pronounced extremist views, connections, and background who in ordinary times and circumstances would probably not have been nominated for President-let alone elected-but for the great unpopularity of both the outgoing George W. Bush Republican Administration; the ongoing Iraq War for which no end was seen; and the perceived incompetence of the Bush Administration.

Despite the anti-Bush/anti-Republican tide in 2008-a political tide in retrospect as strong as any tide could be-John McCain, the Republican Presidential candidate still won twenty-two states: a testament to the enduring strength of conservative Republican principles of government in even the worst of times. Also note that in 1996-the Bill Clinton re-election year when he remained quite popular-the losing Republican Presidential candidate, Kansas US Senator, Bob Dole, still won twenty states.

Judging from the results from both 1996 and 2008- obviously not good years to be a Republican running for national office-a Republican candidate running for President even in the worst of years, can reasonably under normal circumstances look forward to a floor of 20-22 states that he/she will capture in their attempt to win the White House. A fundamental purpose then of Red State Nation by encouraging Republican and conservative voters to relocate from Democrat-majority states to Republican-majority states-or to current "tossup" states in order to flip them to Republican majority states-is to increase and expand the size and depth of the Republicans' Red State "firewall" from its present 20-22 states to perhaps say: 25-26 states, if not larger.

If the Republican Party can build-and maintain-a 25-26 (or larger) state firewall even in the worst of Republican years, it must force the Democrats to work that much harder-and spend that much more money-in order to win a national election. Encouraging Republican and conservative voters to move from states such as California, New York, Illinois, New Jersey, and Maryland, etc.-states which in a normal national election year-the Republican Presidential candidate has little hope of winning-to other and nearby states to these such as: Arizona, New Mexico, Nevada, Colorado, Missouri, Indiana, Ohio, Pennsylvania, and Virginia (among still even others)-the Republican Party's firewall of Red states in a Presidential Election year could be greatly expanded, and could even come close to-if not pass-the 270 Electoral Votes necessary for victory.

Red State Nation as a project and concept if implemented on a large scale with mass conservative participation across the nation will greatly help to address and correct the Republican Party's growing national electoral imbalance that led to Obama's election-at least for a time. However as previously noted the Republican Party must, and more effectively outreach to-and encourage participation by-Hispanic voters, and also Caucasian women. Grooming good Hispanic candidates for national office such as former Florida US Senator Mel Martinez, current Florida US Senator Marco Rubio-plus conservative white women such as (former) Alaska Governor Sarah Palin (as well as former McCain 2008 VP candidate)-will certainly help. A proactive Hispanic outreach will certainly assist the GOP in states such as Florida, Texas, and the other states in the South-West. With an active Red State Nation, plus greatly expanded participation by both Hispanics and white women, the Republican party will be well on its way to again become the dominant political party in America.

As of this writing, the population of the United States is above 300 million people. It is estimated that by the year 2050, the US population will exceed 400 million-perhaps as many as 450 million. The Hispanic population and the African-American population in the United States is increasing at a significantly faster rate than is the white population. The Republican Party-and the conservative movement-must attract and retain at least a moderate percentage of these new Hispanic and black voters which these large population increases will create over the next 40 years. There is no alternative but to do so. If the Republican Party remains-or at least is universally perceived-as a whites only enclave, it will become swallowed up and overwhelmed by the sheer weight of numbers of new Hispanic, black, and other non-white new voters and citizens which will be created by the inevitable increases of population within these groups.

An effective Red State Nation project which generates and maintains a process across the nation by which large numbers of conservative and Republican-minded voters emigrate from the strong, consistently-Democratic voting states into either the "tossup" category states, or the "Red" or Republican majority states to strengthen the Republican Party's control of the Electoral College-will help for a time-but probably not for long-10 or 20 years by itself at most. The Republican Party's gain of strength in the Electoral College resulting from an effective Red State Nation will inevitably too be overwhelmed by the sheer crush of numbers and demographic changes which will come from the continuing increases in America's non-white population, and America's emergence as a majority non-white nation.

Several states that I encourage conservative emigration to are true "swing" states. For instance, most of them fluctuated wildly in the Presidential Elections of 1992, 1996, 2000, 2004, 2008, 2012, and 2016 in their support for Democratic President Clinton in 1992 and 1996; Republican President Bush in 2000 and 2004; again, for Democrat President Obama in 2008 and 2012, and lastly for President Trump in 2016. States such as Nevada, Ohio, Colorado, and Florida all fluctuated in these different election years in that they all delivered their Electoral Votes between Presidents Clinton, Bush, Obama, and Trump. Missouri for one, fluctuated from Democrat Clinton to Republican Bush, but not again switch to the Democrat Obama in 2008, but instead went to Republicans McCain, Romney and Trump as Missouri remained GOP in both 2012 and 2016.

It is particularly toss-up states such as these that Red State Nation is intended to assist. With the infusion of Republicans and conservatives into these states from their former homes in Democrat-majority states, it should greatly help to transform these former toss-up states to consistent Republican-voting "Red states." In doing so, Republican victory in national elections every four years will become much more consistent and certain.

Another example of the relationship between US demographic and population trends and the Electoral College was a Fox News broadcast on August 11, 2009, which announced that the US Government in the 2010 Census was going to count illegal aliens for the purposes of population and congressional representation. In the same broadcast, it was further stated that the decision to count illegal immigrants could represent a net gain to California of as many as nine additional Electoral Votes in the Electoral College. Several other states in the South West were likewise anticipated to experience a population increase from the 2010 Census resulting from the inclusion of the population of illegal aliens residing there-two of them: Texas, and Arizona are consistent Republican-voting states in national elections which will likewise probably experience a net increase of Electoral Votes in the Electoral College.

However, the addition of nine Electoral Votes to California's already high total of 55 (in the 2008 Presidential Election) would give the State of California alone-a regularly-voting Democratic state in national Presidential elections-64 Electoral Votes out of the necessary 270 to win. Such a development has grave implications for the nation. A stronger argument for the defense of the Red State Nation concept can hardly be made. Republicans and conservatives in California would do much to assist their country in this great struggle to stave off socialism in America by leaving California, moving to any one of several nearby states thereby increasing overall Republican political strength in these alternate states-and in the Electoral College. Again, if this were done, this Republican and conservative emigration from California would act as a counterweight to these additional California Electoral Votes for the Democrats resulting from illegal immigration.

There are many thousands of conservatives who currently reside in California and who unfortunately due to weight of numbers are still too few to capture California's many Electoral Votes for the Republican party in a Presidential Election. Republicans and conservative voters in California can do more for the cause of conservatism and freedom in America-and for the nation as a whole-by moving to one of the nearby states. It does not appear that the GOP and conservative voters will be in a position to win any statewide election in California any time soon with the millions of illegal immigrants who are now permitted to register both for drivers' licenses, and to register to vote. The two million vote plus majority for Democrat Hillary Clinton in the 2016 Presidential Election is proof how out of reach the GOP is now to win a statewide election in California. It is far better for these conservative and GOP voters-both for themselves and for the nation as a whole-to join the Red State Nation and move to another state. Just a small portion of California's present population of regular Republican and conservative voters effectively distributed among the Mountain-West and Southwest states near California: i.e.., states such as Arizona, New Mexico, Nevada, Colorado, etc., would likely transform any or all of these states into firm, consistent Republican-voting states in national elections. Despite the likely impending increase in Democratic California's votes in the Electoral College, participation, and contribution by California's conservatives to the Red State Nation effort will greatly assist the country.

As stated previously, Tea Party members can be both among the most enthusiastic émigrés themselves in vacating from Blue states, as well as powerful advocates and volunteers in the building of a Red State Nation. I would like to see the many thousands of Tea party volunteers from hundreds of Tea Parties across this country; those wonderful volunteers who gathered together on those magical days of April 15, 2009, and also on July 4, 2009-plus on other occasions-to gather again; to volunteer; and to help their conservative brethren pack and move from their current homes in high-tax Democrat/left states. In doing this, they would help free the émigrés themselves and this nation from socialism, confiscation, and oppression. Helping their conservative neighbors pack and move from high-tax, liberal-left, Democrat states to more conservative Republican states is no less a protest against "taxation without representation," and in my view is a far more effective one.

The Obama Presidency in spawning a patriotic resistance in the Tea Party movement, a movement of ordinary citizen activists-many of whom never previously demonstrated an interest in public and political affairs before-is of course a movement that I both greatly admire and sympathize with. It is also a movement that I hope endures and survives beyond the Obama Presidency which gave it birth, and I trust that it shall. I further hope that the Tea Party movement also greatly contributes to a vigorous involvement with its large benefactor, the Donald Trump Administration, once it safely survived 8 years of the Obama Presidency, with its accompanying IRS harassment to boot.

I would like to see a substantial interaction between the broad elements of the national Tea Party movement and the Republican Party in the many states. Former Alaska Governor and 2008 Republican VP Candidate, Sarah Palin, has called for much the same thing. Such an integration can only serve to benefit both the Tea Party movement and the Republican Party, and greatly contribute to Republican and conservative electoral success. Also, a substantial influx of conservative, anti-Obama, and anti-socialism activists can only serve to benefit and improve the Republican Party as a whole and keep it honest to its conservative principles.

At its fringes, the national Tea Party movement undoubtedly has some of the more extreme elements of the conservative movement: i.e.. Obama "Birthers," nullification proponents, secessionists, etc. At its core, the national Tea Party movement is a pro-American, pro-Constitution, reform-minded movement with people strongly opposed to the socialist direction of the country and the Obama Presidency. As the broad elements of the national Tea Party movement integrate themselves with the national Republican Party to combine themselves to form a broad anti-Obama/anti-socialism alliance, how much the fringe elements of the Tea Party movement "go along for the ride" is certainly subject for speculation. Many of them have always been on the fringe of American political life-and seem destined to remain there.

It is a testament to their love of our country and their collective hope for its future that so many thousands of conservative Americans-as well as others-gathered across the country for their Tea Party protests on both 4/15/2009, 7/4/2009, and 4/15/2010. However symbolic protests against taxation without representation are - while fine; they still are symbolic.. It is much more significant to do more against taxation without representation than just to symbolically protest such as by participating in an actual project such as Red State Nation in assisting freedom-loving Amsticans to flee socialism and high-taxation in the quest for low taxation and freedom. Participating in Red State Nation takes tangible and strong action against taxation without representation, and if enough conservatives participate, deals it perhaps a fatal blow and which benefits everyone, and the nation as a whole. I call upon all Tea Party participants-of which I am one-particularly those in the worst Democrat-majority high-tax states such as California, Illinois, and New York to go beyond symbolism and to support Red State Nation. The fundamental concept of Red State Nation, i.e.. to utilize Republican and conservative electoral and political strength in the most effective manner in order to win and maintain control of the nation's Electoral College, is a concept that is compatible with the broad aims and message of the national Tea Party movement.

In addition, I argue that Red State Nation is the necessary and logical next step beyond the Tea Party movement. In saying this, I reiterate my admiration for the Tea Party movement and for its many thousands of patriotic members, of which I am one myself. I am simply saying that the Tea Party movement by itself does not go far enough to address the securing of consistent Electoral College victory for Constitution-loving, conservative Republican Presidential candidates. Nor is the Tea Party movement as it is presently set up structured to assist conservative Republican victory more fully in the Electoral College. Collectively between the dark Blue states of California, New York, Illinois, and New Jersey, there are literally hundreds if not more of individual Tea Party chapters, comprising of many thousands of members. Many of these Tea Party members among these chapters in these particular dark Blue states are undoubtedly among the most spirited and dedicated Tea Party members that you could find anywhere. The umbrella organization, Tea Party Express, is even headquartered in California.

However, the presence of maybe even thousands of spirited and dedicated Tea Party members in these darkest of Blue states does not alter the fact that these states are dark Blue for a reason: numbers, and that these Tea Party activists, plus the other conservatives and regular Republican voters in the state are, regardless of their passion, unfortunately still insignificant in terms of collective numbers as opposed to the numbers of Democrats and leftists in the state. Again, we are in a war with the Democratic left for the soul and control of this country. If we want to save this country from the left, we must govern our conduct accordingly to achieve that end. Just as moving and positioning pieces on a chessboard, our fellow conservatives and Republican voters in these present dark Blue states should seriously contemplate a move to the more conservative, Republican-friendly, or one of the tossup states previously identified if they are in the position to do so. Moving out of these dark Blue states would be in their individual best interests, plus that of the nation as a whole. The Tea Party in these states can greatly contribute and be most effective by their state members also moving who are in the position to do so, but also by assisting the others.

President George W. Bush left office in 2009 with less than a 30% approval rating in some polls. His great unpopularity-and that of the Iraq War for which he was entirely responsible-were critical factors in the election of Barack Obama. Bush's final Presidential legacy will likely remain unsettled and murky for many years-perhaps decades-before it begins to perhaps improve as in the instance of

President Harry S. Truman. Bush's great personal unpopularity, especially in the latter years of his 2nd Term, as well as his singlehanded, stubborn, and seemingly obsessive defense and championing of the equally-unpopular War in Iraq; greatly damaged his own Presidency. It also of course has greatly damaged his legacy and his own Rep3ublican Party in 2008, which had already withstood serious electoral defeats in the mid-term elections of 2006.

Thanks to Bush's unpopularity, plus that of his Iraq War, the national Republican Party almost overnight went from a powerful majority party in control of both houses of Congress plus the Presidency, to a virtual impotent minority party in charge of nothing following the 2008 and the accession of Barack Obama to the Presidency. In greatly wounding his own Republican Party and in paving the way by his actions and unpopularity to Obama's 2008 election, Bush most of all greatly wounded the country. The Bush-less Republican Party exited the 2008 elections with but 40 US Senators and greatly outnumbered as well in the US House of Representatives, and lastly very much out-gunned to attempt to defend the nation from the socialist onslaught from both Obama and his rejuvenated Democratic Party. Seemingly the Texans had better odds at the Alamo against the Mexicans in 1836; likewise, Custer at the Little Big Horn against Sitting Bull than those faced by the Republicans in Congress in 2009.

However, facing again the future of American as a majority non-white nation-plus that of the Republican Party and the conservative movement-one can still take many positive elements from the Presidency of George W. Bush-most of which were greatly overshadowed by the mistakes that he made. Throughout his entire 8-year Presidency, several African-American members were appointed to serve in his Cabinet including 2 different ones: Colin Powell and Condoleezza Rice-for the all-important post of Secretary of State during Bush's entire tenure. Colin Powell ultimately abandoned the GOP to become a strong Obama supporter, Obama of course being the first African-American President. Likewise, prominent Hispanic members such as Attorney General, Eliot Gonzalez, served during President

Bush's 2nd Term. In addition, President Bush nominated several well-qualified Hispanic and African-American judicial candidates for the Federal judiciary. Finally, President Bush encouraged and actually supported distinguished African-American and Hispanic Republican candidates in several prominent election races across the country including Lynn Swann in Pennsylvania; Michael Steele in Maryland; Ken Blackwell in Ohio; and Mel Martinez in Florida.

For all of the good however that President Bush did to broaden and expand the base of the Republican Party by expanding opportunities and participation for Hispanics and African-Americans, it is unfortunate that much of it was otherwise overshadowed by mistakes that he made, plus the unpopularity of the Iraq War. Now that President Bush has as of this writing left the stage, and his great personal unpopularity-plus that of the Iraq War to which he was closely identified-is no longer a millstone around the neck of the Republican Party and the conservative movement-we would be wise to recall and also to reflect on the good that President Bush attempted to do, and succeeded in doing, particularly in his profound desire to expand opportunities and participation. We Republicans and conservatives must follow the lead of President Bush and aggressively reach out, embrace, and join with our conservative Hispanic and African-American brethren of like mind, and make common cause with them. A growing conservative movement in this country, hand-in-hand with an expanding Republican Party which maintains and open door with a welcome mat towards Hispanics and African-Americans of like mind is a positive force which cannot be denied. A thriving Red State Nation project of redistribution of conservative and Republican popular, electoral strength to those states where it would make it most effective and potent, would make this positive force all the stronger.

In the necessary pursuit of support-and votes-from the nation's Hispanics, the Republican Party and its conservative allies must effectively come to grips with-and satisfactorily resolve-what I would identify as the "Hispanic Paradox." We Republicans and conservatives must embrace and vigorous strive to receive the political support-and concurrently deny it to our leftist enemies-of American Hispanics while at the same time continue to combat the concept of blanket amnesty for those illegal immigrants-many of them of course of Hispanic origin-who have already entered the country. Obviously, we have yet to overcome the Hispanic Paradox, but yet we must do so for the future of the country. Republicans and conservatives who stand for the rule of law such as President Trump will always suffer the lack of support of many Hispanics who demand blanket amnesty for those illegal immigrants who require it to obtain citizenship. The Democratic left who allowed the illegals into the country in the first place by refusing to secure the US-Mexican border in order to keep them out would only too readily grant all illegal immigrants blanket amnesty or anything else required and/or demanded in order to get these millions of illegals currently in the country onto the voter rolls, and regularly pulling the Democratic lever in the voting booth. Many former immigrants who both entered the United States legally-and pursued US citizenship legally-may perhaps appreciate and support the GOP position in support of the rule of law and opposed to blanket amnesty for illegals, however probably not all of them do.

Our leftist and socialist adversaries in the Democratic Party are very mindful of our dilemma presented to us by the Hispanic Paradox and they have done-as evidenced by actions and statements by prominent Democrats during the entire Sonya S. Sotomayer confirmation process to the US Supreme Court in 2009-and will continue to cause as much trouble for conservatives and the Republican Party with American Hispanics by simply claiming that conservatives and the Republican Party are simply racist and anti-Hispanic. Given the decline of Hispanic support for the Republican Party from the 2004 to the 2008 Presidential Elections, the Democrats have achieved success in causing trouble for the Republican Party with American Hispanics. The leftist anti-Hispanic accusations against Republicans are indeed ludicrous when one considers how it was the GOP who ultimately nominated and elected outstanding US Senate candidates such as Marco Rubio in Florida in 2010, and again, Mel Martinez earlier, also in Florida. These outrageous anti-Hispanic racism accusations against Republicans and conservatives by the Democrats are not true and never have been, but as long as there continues to remain a Hispanic Paradox to overcome, we will continue to remain on the defensive, must continue to explain and defend ourselves against unfair and untrue accusations; and lastly will have to continue to fight and scratch for all possible Hispanic political support. President Trump's efforts in the 2016 election campaign, coupled with his and the GOP's minority outreach efforts-with the committed assistance of of GOP minority conservatives such as Dr. Ben Carson-did show some improvement and continued promise for the same.

The support of American Hispanics is the most coveted political plum on the tree today. The Democratic left is well aware that one of the primary factors for the 2008 Obama Presidential victory-not to mention his margin of victory-was the great increase in the percentage of support that he received from American Hispanics as opposed to that received by their 2004 Presidential candidate, Democratic US Senator John Kerry of Massachusetts. Obama in 2008 received approximately 69% of the support of American Hispanics while in 2004, Kerry received but 55% of it. This great upsurge in the amount of American Hispanic support for Obama in 2008 is clearly critical as to the results of both elections, as the other percentage differences in both the support by white Americans and by African-Americans received by Obama in 2008 as opposed to that received by Kerry in 2004, are marginal at best. Though there was a slight uptick in African-American support for Obama in 2008 (96%), over that already-large percentage won by Senator Kerry in 2004 (91%), African-American pride in Obama as the first African-American major party Presidential nominee clearly is a primary reason for the uptick.

The Democratic Party today as dominated by its extreme left wing is a Party committed to socialism, to government dominance in the nation's economic system. Their wish-and goal-is to transform America into a socialistic nation. As already noted, the great mass of American Hispanics share with us conservative Republican principles and have no sympathies-or inclinations-towards socialism. The left has but a tenuous grasp on the sympathies of American Hispanics most of which results from their bogus and fraudulent claims of anti-Hispanic racism on the part of American conservatives and the Republican Party due to the lack of resolution of the issues of illegal immigration and the Hispanic Paradox in a way that is reasonable and satisfactory for all. With these issues retired, there would remain no phony or artificial barriers to prevent a consistent and significant portion of American Hispanics to support Republican candidates and the Republican Party, consistent with the inherent conservative principles of many of them.

Geraldo Rivera, the famous Hispanic journalist, and news commentator recited a quotation attributed to late President Ronald Reagan on a Fox News broadcast on 8/3/2009 while describing and endorsing his own latest book on the Hispanic experience in America. Rivera quoted Reagan as saying that the Hispanic people are Republicans waiting to be discovered, and that "we Republicans must discover them." President Reagan is the author of many verbal gems that are widely quoted and cited, and this one presented by Rivera is no less valuable-or prophetic-as any other. If we who are Republicans do discover those same qualities in the Hispanic people that we value in ourselves: love of work and enterprise; love of family; love of country; and love of God-then the great mass of Hispanic people will finally be discovered and recognized as the fellow Republicans which they should be and embraced as such by us all. When that moment comes, our nation is finally safe from socialism; conservative principles will be preserved and become dominant; and the Republican Party should not lose another national election.

CHAPTER 5:

THE EMERGING REPUBLICAN MAJORITY.

Following the Election of Republican President Richard Nixon in 1968, a distinguished Republican strategist (who served on the Nixon election campaign) named Kevin Phillips authored a fine, definitive book titled: "The Emerging Republican Majority. (1)" Phillips' work in many respects pre-dates my current effort here. Phillips' central thesis in "The Emerging Republican Majority" at the time was that the national Republican Party was virtually assured of an era of continued national electoral dominance in that it had an electoral stranglehold of a sufficient number of states at the time in the Mountain West, Mid-West, and the South which the Democratic Party could not then challenge.

The results of the two Nixon elections in both 1968, and particularly 1972 in which President Nixon won re-election against South Dakota Democratic US Senator George S. McGovern by capturing the Electoral Votes of 49 of the 50 states (McGovern winning only the State of Massachusetts, plus the District of Columbia) certainly argued strongly in support of the Phillips thesis of an emerging Republican majority. Again, in my view, Mr. Phillips' central thesis at that time remains essentially true today. In the intervening 50 years since the publication of "The Emerging Republican Majority" and today in 2019, there has been no great explosion of liberalism states in such as Idaho, Wyoming, Utah, and say, Alabama and Mississippi.

Instead, the one principal variable in many of these states-particularly the Western ones such as Colorado, Utah, Nevada, Arizona, and New Mexico-states that for the most part Kevin Phillips included as part of his "Emerging Republican Majority" is the great increase in the last 40 years in their non-white, specifically Hispanic population. The remaining Caucasian population in many of these states-a smaller percentage of the whole population today than existed in 1969-is for the most part no less conservative, and no less disinclined to vote for the Republican Presidential candidate in national elections than 50 years ago. Again, these changes in demographics show clearly why both the conservative movement and the Republican Party today must make every effort to embrace and to include within our ranks as much of the growing Hispanic population as is sympathetic to our conservative beliefs and principles and would wish to join with us. Particularly for the crucial Western states that were previously a part of the emerging Republican majority but now with rapidly accelerating Hispanic population growth, we can literally leave no stone unturned to find the last sympathetic Hispanic voter.

Again however, many of these Hispanics in these Western states are not American citizens but are in fact, illegal immigrants, and many of them in fact have been voting in American elections with the full encouragement of the Democratic Party.

The election results of the 1976 Presidential Election when little-known former Georgia Democratic-Governor Jimmy Carter narrowly defeated Republican President Gerald Ford did not in my view represent a clear repudiation of the Phillips thesis of an emerging Republican majority though Carter's election might obviously seem on the surface to represent such a repudiation. The reason for this is that President Carter was a unique Democratic Presidential candidate at the time and whose uniqueness as such, greatly served to skewer the Phillips electoral model for Republican victory as highlighted by his book.

First of all, Carter was well-known as a moderate in a Democratic Party then (as today) primarily dominated by both liberals and ultra-liberals. Somewhat amusing perhaps now is the perception that Carter's reputation then as a moderate Democrat was much more pronounced than his reputation is now for being one as he is now consistently viewed as a very left-wing ex-President given his current views of favoring rapprochement with North Korea, Cuba, and the Arab terrorist group, Hamas

Second of all, he was a Southerner in a Democratic Party up until then nationally dominated by Northerners named McGovern, Kennedy, Humphrey, etc. It was well-publicized at the time that a Carter victory would put the first Southerner in the White House since prior to the Civil War. In the 1976 Presidential Election, Carter as the Democratic candidate carried several several Southern states including his own native Georgia which almost certainly would have supported the Republican candidate President Ford in conformity to the Phillips electoral model In Emerging Republican Majority had the Democratic party in place of Carter nominated a typical Norther, liberal candidate as the Presidential nominee such as Walter Mondale, the Democratic US Senator from Minnesota whom Carter did choose as his Vice Presidential candidate that year. It is speculative, but doubtful that Mondale as the nominee would have won the same states that Carter did.

I reiterate that the Phillips electoral model in the Emerging Republican Majority were skewered by the elections results of 1976 and the election of President Carter. Many white southerners that year-particularly conservative ones-voted for Democratic candidate Carter for both the historical aspects of his candidacy, and also as a matter of "Southern Pride." In a more traditional Presidential Election where the Democratic candidate was a typical Northern liberal, many of Carter's southern white voters would have voted instead for the more conservative Republican candidate, President Ford in conformity with the Phillips electoral model. The terms "Red States" and "Blue States" signifying Republican-voting and Democratic-voting states had not yet come into vogue in 1976. As the terms are understood today, there is little dispute that Georgia is properly character-ized as a "Red State;" ie. A Republican-voting one. Yet, Jimmy Car-ter-native son though he is-carried the State of Georgia in both the Presidential Elections of 1976 (against Republican candidate, President Gerald R. Ford), and also 1980 (against Republican candidate, Ronald W. Reagan). Democrats in 2016 boasted that they would soon turn Georgia "blue," and in fact for much of the 2016 Presidential Campaign the Democrats extensively campaigned in Georgia to flip it for the 2016 Clinton-Kane Democratic ticket, but Georgia did in fact remain "red" and by a comfortable margin. Again, it was extensive Hispanic resettlement into Georgia prior to the 2016 election which raised the issue, and nothing else.

In the 1980 Presidential Election, Georgia was the only Southern state carried by Carter, and also, the only state that could certainly be identified as a Red State as Carter won but a total of six states in his 1980 landslide re-election loss to Republican Ronald Reagan, who won a total of 44 states. The 1976 Carter election aberration in the Phillips electoral model was emphatically rectified by the results of the 1980 Presidential Election. It is speculative yet interesting to contemplate the election results of the 1976 Presidential Election were Jimmy Carter then widely-viewed as the pronounced leftist that he is today, rather than the attractive southern moderate, and as such the viable alternative to centrist voters to both northern liberals and old-style southern politicians such as George Wallace with an anti-civil rights reputation. If Jimmy Carter then had the leftist rep-utation that he does now, would he have nonetheless won the 1976 Presidential Election? Would southern pride still have trumped the Phillips electoral model? Carter may still have won his own state of Georgia in 1976-as indeed he did he did in the 1980 election -after a widely-perceived failed four-year Presidency. But would he have won any of the other southern states which he had carried in the 1976 election? All are today-just as Georgia is-clearly identified as "Red" or pro-Republican voting states. His victory over President Ford as it was in 1976 was a narrow one, and a switch of 2 or 3 of the other southern states carried by Carter over to Ford would have flipped the 1976 Presidential Election over to President Ford. This analysis highlights very well how ex-Georgia Governor, Democrat Jimmy Carter successful election to the Presidency in 1976 was in many respects an aberration, and as such skewered the Phillips electoral model of a Republican-majority nation which has stood well the test of time. The "Red" states captured by President George W. Bush in both his initial 2000 effort, and in his 2004 re-election effort-both successful-greatly followed the Phillips Republican victory electoral map model in both elections.

As to the state of Georgia, Democrats in 2016 boasted that they would soon turn Georgia "Blue," and in fact for much of the 2016 Presidential Election, Democrats extensively campaigned in Georgia to flip it for the Clinton-Kane Democratic ticket, but Georgia did in fact remain "Red" and by a comfortable margin in 2016. Again, it was extensive Hispanic resettlement in Georgia prior to the 2016 election which raised the issue, and nothing else.

Had the political reputation of Jimmy Carter not drifted far leftwards of that which he enjoyed in the mid-1970's, he may very well today be described as a "Blue Dog Democrat"-a term not in prominence in the mid-1970's. The so-called "Blue Dog Democrats" are the counterpart in the Democratic Party to the "RINOS" (Republicans In Name Only) in the Republican Party. For the most part though not entirely, "Blue Dog Democrats" are found in the Republican or "Red States" and are much more conservative-particularly on social issues-than are the typical leftist Democrats to be found in particularly the darkest Blue states such as Massachusetts, New York, New Jersey, Illinois, and California.

In many of the southern states following the 2004 Presidential Election in which George W. Bush (once again) swept all eleven states of the old Southern Confederacy, the Democratic Party made a determined effort to increase its influence and Congressional representation in the region. In 2006, with President Bush's popularity in decline and the anti-Bush reaction in full swing, the Democrats captured 30 seats in the US House of Representatives previously held by the Republicans. Those Democrats who did so in Congressional Districts won by President Bush in 2004 and/or 2000-particularly in southern states-have been termed "Blue Dog Democrats."

In many instances, these Blue Dog Democrats won their seats in conservative, normally Republican-voting districts by being particularly critical of President Bush. In some instances, even, the Blue Dog Democratic candidate ran as the more conservative alternative to their Republican counterpart in the race. Some of the Blue Dogs may have even run as "anti-Bush conservatives" with very little reference to their actual Democratic Party affiliation. As the Republicans have learned with their "RINO" office holders-particularly those in northern or "Blue" Democratic states (such as US Senators Arlen Spector of PA-previously a "RINO" Republican, then a pro-Obama Democrat (now deceased); both Maine US Senators, Republicans Susan Collins and Olympia Snowe, and former Rhode Island US Senator, Republican Lincoln Chaffee), the Democrats have likewise learned that their Blue Dogs, particularly those in the southern, conservative-voting, and any other normally-Republican voting districts, are really a double-edged sword or mixed-blessing at best. It has remained the intransigence of many of the conservative Blue Dog Democrats in Congress which had prevented the stampede of much of President Obama's leftist agenda in 2009 through Congress such as nationalized health care. Perhaps an alternative name for the Blue Dog Democrats would be "DINOS" (i.e.. Democrats In Name Only).

As can be seen by the difficult Democratic efforts to enact the Obama socialistic legislative agenda in 2009, the 2006 and 2008 election attempts to expand their control of Congress by electing conservative, Blue Dog Democrats, particularly those from "Red" states-has not helped the Democratic Party much. It can perhaps be acknowledged that Blue Dog Democrats in the 2009 US Congress performed a great service to the nation by standing with the outnumbered and out-gunned Republicans in that Congress to provide a firewall against Obama's socialism. Yes, to be fair, these Blue Dogs should be commended for at least that.

However, this praise-however faint-for the Blue Dog Democrats should only go so far. Blue Dogs or not, they are still Democrats, and they still call themselves Democrats, so they should not be entirely trusted. Again, giving credit to where credit is due to those Blue Dog Democrats who have stood firm against Obama's socialism, conservative and Republican voters-particularly in the Red states-should always choose to support a Republican candidate for office over even a Blue Dog Democrat-no matter how attractive, persuasive, and seemingly-conservative the Blue Dog may be. If a Blue Dog Democrat has enough scruples and is sufficiently-principled to stand in the path of a left-wing President's socialistic agenda such as Obama's, then he or she should have sufficient scruples and principles to change their political party affiliation to Republican. If the Red State Nation is to succeed and to be a bulwark to protect this nation from Obama-style, leftist/socialist Democratic rule, there can be no room for Blue Dog Democrats in the Red states. The 2010 and 2012 Congressional Elections should have represented as indeed the 2010 midterms surely did, an "electoral correction' in removing hopefully, dozens of Blue Dog Democrats from conservative, Republican districts where they were elected from and never properly should have been in the first place and were it not for an anti-Bush hysteria in frequent instances, most likely would not have been.

As evidenced by the 2000 and 2004 Presidential Elections-particularly the 2000 one which for all intents and purposes was a tie-the United States can be-and sometimes is-referred to a "50/50 nation:" i.e.. half Democrat/half Republican, or perhaps half conservative/ half liberal. It is not really that way; it just seems that way. Again, in poll after poll, America is indisputably a center-right nation. The 2008 Presidential Election in which Democrat Barack Hussein Obama, a certified leftist Democrat with a pronounced socialist agenda won his convincing Electoral College victory after winning the Democratic

Presidential nomination against great odds-can be viewed-and is by this writer-as an aberration-simply a result of a confluence of a number of distinct factors. These factors included: the then great unpopularity of outgoing President George W. Bush-again primarily due to the great unpopularity of his Iraq War, the sharp 2008 recession for which the Democrats themselves were as much responsible for as any; and lastly, Obama's masterful deception of the electorate on the campaign trail by his adoption of pro-Republican and conservative rhetoric and disguising his true intentions. With the first two of the preceding factors, any Democratic Presidential candidate would likely have won the 2008 Presidential Election. The proof in the pudding is the fact that Barack Hussein Obama did win it the most extreme leftist Democratic candidate imaginable; a candidate who in ordinary circumstances would have hardly been nominated, let alone elected.

As a nation we derive dubious (at best) benefit from the perception that we are in fact a 50/50 nation, and that we are governed accordingly. Political acrimony between Democrats and Republicans; the left and the right, as is evident in the first year of Obama's term as he has struggled to enact his socialist agenda, is as sharp and in many instances as virulent-as it has ever been. Many Americans-including those on opposite ends of the political spectrum-do not like this acrimony, and the political gridlock which results from it with the inability to seemingly get anything accomplished. In my view, the leftist Democrats are unable to govern nationally, and I state this at a time when they indeed control both Houses of the US Congress, as well as the Presidency. The Democrats are a political party based on the left, whose core-essence is a leftist-socialist party, and again the country as a whole is center-right. As has already been seen, the Democratic Party even though it at present controls Congress in 2009, instead arguably controls nothing in that it is in the words of Lincoln: "a house divided against itself." This is again because a significant minority of the Democrats in Congress are the Blue Dog Democrats-many from Red States-who did not favor Obama's socialist-leftist agenda.

In summary, the Democratic Party is truly unable to govern nationally both because the country as a whole is center/right in temperament rather than leftist-socialist, and also because regardless of the numbers elected, most Congressional candidates that the Democrats can elect from the Red states would be Blue Dog Democrats-just as conservative in most instances (by political necessity) as any Republican. It would then seem that the country's political system should be as a ripe plum ready to fall into the Republican Party's hands. Nothing, however, is ever that easy. Remember that the Electoral College artificially inflates the national strength of the Democratic Party in national Presidential elections-particularly again in such large and critical states as California, Illinois, New York, and New Jersey because these states as they are populous, have many Republican and conservative voters in them, however yet an insufficient number in each but to rarely carry the state in a national election. It has been commented by many as a result of the 2016 Presidential Election that the Democratic Party is really but a bi-coastal Party leaving much of the nation's interior in the firm grip of the GOP. A project such as Red State Nation which proposes to facilitate the transfer of these excessive conservative voters in the large Democratic states to current Republican-voting or Red states, or to current "swing" states to transform them into new, consistent Red states in the Electoral College is just what is needed to combat the current artificial inflation of the Democratic Party's strength in the Electoral College.

It is the current inflation of the Democratic Party's strength in the Electoral College-brought about by the current lack of a project such as proposed Red State Nation to resolve it-which in turn greatly contributes to the 50/50 nation perception, as well as to the political gridlock in Washington which ensnares us, as well as infuriates nearly all. That is correct, the 50/50 nation perception is an artificial one as well and is very much enhanced by the Democratic Party's artificially inflated strength by the Electoral College, and the political gridlock unnecessarily follows from both. As can be then seen, Red State Nation cures all of this; it is a game changer.

The influx of conservatives from primarily Democratic states where their votes are discounted, and which only serve to artificially inflate Democratic Party strength in the Electoral College, will in turn assist existing Republicans and conservatives in current Red or tossup states to defeat existing "Blue Dog Democrats" in these states and help to prevent both their reelection and re-appearance there. The Red State Nation which is in effect a national re-balancing of conservative and Republican voters in the Red or Republican states-and to the tossup states also to help "flip" them into Red-is the necessary concentration of conservative political power in this country which is needed to assure the ascendancy of conservative political principles and ideals and the defeat of Democratic left-wing socialism. In this concentration of conservative of conservative political power by this unleashing of conservative political strength, the 50/50 nation is broken; the Electoral College will no longer artificially inflate the political strength of the leftist Democrats; and the re-balancing of the conservative movement's political strength in this country-and in Washington-will more closely approximate the center-right nation that it consistently polls as. A Red State Nation project then is clearly a re-balancing for not only the conservative movement and Republican Party, but also for the nation as a whole.

With the Republican Party's and conservative movement's true politic ascendancy unleashed by a Red State Nation effort, the balance will be tipped from a 50/50 nation; gridlock in Washington can be broken, and loud volume and acrimony lessens as well. The leftist-socialist Democratic Party can be effectively relegated to 2nd place status. A particularly effective Red State Nation effort to increase conservative and Republican emigration to Pennsylvania from the states of New Jersey, and especially New York, will go far to insure the Democratic Party's permanent 2nd place status in national elections. The conversion of Pennsylvania into a legitimate, consistently-Republican voting "Red" state from its current status as a tossup/weak "Blue" state is both quite attainable, and very nearly by itself a game changer in Red/Blue state Electoral College strategy. Not even Kevin Phillips in the "Emerging Republican Majority" elaborated on the possibility of Pennsylvania being a consistent Republican state. So much the better for Republican prospects today.

Make no mistake; an effective Red State Nation effort can transform Pennsylvania into a consistent Republican-voting state-much like neighboring Ohio and West Virginia-and every effort should be made to make a "Red" Pennsylvania a reality. A permanent flip of Pennsylvania into a consistently voting Republican or Red state will relegate the Democrats in the Electoral College to simply consistently winning the states of New York, New Jersey, the various small New England states (with the possible exception of New Hampshire), Illinois, and the West Coast/Pacific states of California, Oregon, Washington, and Hawaii-scarcely 18 states total, and would hardly justify an argument in defense of the notion of a 50/50 nation from the Democratic perspective.

In addition, with a successful Red State Nation effort, most of these Democrat or "Blue" states would suffer population-and eventual electoral-attrition as conservatives and Republicans vacated these states and emigrated to Red states or the designated toss-up states to advance the Red State Nation effort as indeed at this writing, many of these Blue states are experiencing population attrition. A consistent, energetic Red State Nation effort is necessary to break the electoral and legislative gridlock in Washington, and to tip the nation's balance from a so-called 50/50 nation to one that genuinely reflects the center-right political orientation of the majority of the nation's electorate. And yes, the keystone in the Red State Nation effort is the Keystone State itself, Pennsylvania, and the successful transformation of it into a consistently-voting Red or Republican state; it can-and must-be done.

Pennsylvania while remaining at best (or perhaps worst) a light-Blue state in that it had not been from 1988 to 2016 won by a Republican Presidential candidate since 1988 nonetheless does boast of a substantial and aggressive Republican political minority in the state which has frequently fought the Democratic state governors and the

Democrats in the state legislature to a standstill. Property taxes on the whole-not to mention car insurance rates-are far more attractive in Pennsylvania than they are in neighboring New Jersey. Likewise, sales and income taxes are much more attractive in Pennsylvania than they are in neighboring New York. Conservative and Republican voters in both states-particularly those from southern New Jersey (New Jersey having a north/south divide, much like Pennsylvania's east/ west one)-and also those from upstate New York, would find moving to and living in Pennsylvania a very attractive and affordable alternative than that of remaining where they are at present. Initiating-and maintaining-an energizing and effective effort in both of these states to encourage emigration of Republicans and conservatives to Pennsylvania could result in the movement of many thousands to the Keystone State. Such a movement-once started and if it continues-would go far to quickly overcome the Democrats' advantages in Pennsylvania both by virtue of Eastern Pennsylvania as a whole as previously cited by Rick Santorum, and also Philadelphia's unique situation in particular. The net goal to the entire country in flipping Pennsylvania from light-Blue to consistent- Red would be incalculable.

It is anticipated that even with the launch of an effective, nationwide Red State Nation effort and the resulting movement of conservative and Republican voters from primary Democrat states to both Republican states and tossup states, some states which heretofore had been tightly-contested battlegrounds in recent Presidential Elections will likely remain so. A number of states, particularly in the upper Mid-West which were hotly contested in the Bush 2000 and 2004 elections-and for a time in the Obama 2008 effort-are likely to remain hotly contested in future elections. States such as Iowa, Minnesota, Wisconsin, and Michigan are these states which have been-and are likely to remain hotly-contested at least for a time-in subsequent Presidential Elections. All of these but Minnesota-narrowly-were won by President Trump in 2016. None of these particular MidWestern states were included among those identified by Kevin Phillips as part of his Emerging Republican Majority. A (yet) non-stated goal of Red

State Nation is to solidify the inherent, conservative and Republican character of those states originally identified by Phillips over 40 years ago-most of which-to a greater or lesser extent-retain their same Republican character as observed and identified by Phillips back then in his work. The solidification of the Republican and conservative character of these Red states is the constant infusion of Republican and conservative expatriates from other and pro-Democratic states where their votes were wasted.

The other variable which has influenced the Republican character of many of these states identified by Phillips as Republican-and has eroded to a degree the same Republican character of many of them since the Phillips work-is of course again, that of demographics, specifically the great growth of the influence and the extent of the Hispanic vote in many of these states since 1969 as we have already seen. The goal however of Red State Nation is not simply to once again resurrect a Republican majority of Red states based simply based upon the Phillips model, but to expand the Phillips model. We have already seen this by the extensive discussion on the state of Pennsylvania, again a state certainly not included by Phillips as a part of his Emerging Republican Majority.

An effective Red State Nation effort can also be initiated in the state of New Hampshire, the small New England state, certainly highly-contested-and very narrowly won-in both of the 2000 and 2004 Bush Presidential Elections (in 2000 by Bush, and in 2004 by Democratic candidate, US Senator John Kerry from next-door Massachusetts). All of the rest of New England-particularly neighboring strong Democratic states of Vermont, Massachusetts, and Connecticut-can serve as the feeder states from which Republicans and conservatives can move from to emigrate to New Hampshire. Also, again in 2016, very narrowly won by Democratic candidate Clinton. Also, far upstate New York near Vermont can also contribute Republican and conservative émigrés to New Hampshire's Red State Nation effort. New Hampshire is a beautiful state (as indeed most of the rest of New England is) and has many solid attributes to encourage out-of-state emigration to it, including its lack of a state income tax. The state motto of New Hampshire: "Live Free or Die." is clearly one which resonates with many conservatives. The unique problem which New Hampshire presents is that its many attributes are an ill-kept secret and that unfortunately many Democrats-especially from high-tax Massachusetts-are moving there as well, particularly to southern New Hampshire.

Again, in the instance of New Hampshire, we see an example of Democratic voters leaving an unattractive high-tax area-like the City of Philadelphia, PA (for its suburbs) - which their own foolish, misguided policies have helped to create to move to a new, predominantly Republican, conservative area. As before, the Democrats then attempt to pollute the new area with their leftist-socialist philosophies by not changing them by failing to recognize that it was their own failed leftist policies which corrupted and polluted their previous living environment, and this created and fueled their motivation to move-and to flee their own handiwork Conservatives and Red State Nation must make a concerted effort to preserve New Hampshire's unique conservative and freedom-loving heritage before it is damaged and ultimately destroyed by incoming leftists who fleeing like locusts the fruits of their own foolish handiwork at their previous states of residence such as the alien adversaries in the movie, "Independence Day."

It is unfortunate that we cannot pass an enforceable law which would prohibit-and quarantine-leftist and socialistic Democrats from moving from one of their own "Blue" states such as New York or California, etc. which they have already ruined into other states, particularly traditional Republican and conservative ones such as Florida or New Hampshire, etc. so that the spread and corrosive influence of their policies could be limited, controlled, and quarantined. Clearly such a law, or even an attempt at one, would be unconstitutional, and the very antithesis of freedom, even to those Democratic leftists who would not hesitate to deny freedom to others. Accordingly, if we cannot deny the spread of leftists and their extreme liberal influence by enactments then we must defeat their numbers in the critical states that they attempt to emigrate to Back to New Hampshire, its Electoral Votes- regularly added to those of Pennsylvania, plus those of the more traditional Red states in national elections will make the mountain that much more difficult to climb for the Democratic socialistic-left to once again win a national election in this country. As with Pennsylvania, conservatives and Red State Nation can and must contest the left for political control over New Hampshire and can- and must-prevail in this contest. The future of our country depends upon it.

The battle over the control of America and her destiny with the Democratic left via the Electoral College, if it is to be won by conservative Americans in defense of the nation, its institutions, and Democratic traditions, and especially the fundamental principle of a free market (and non-government-controlled or dominated) economy, must be done by a process as I have described and termed herein as "Red State Nation, "or a process similar. Within the present structure of our constitutional political system, there is no other way. Our Founding Fathers in their wisdom devised the Electoral College as an institution and the process by which we elect our Presidents in the US Constitution at its outset in 1789. From time to time-including in the present-we have heard loud outcries from both the right and the left that the Electoral College as an institution was unfair and/or antiquated and should be either greatly revised and/or abolished. With the Trump electoral victory in 2016, we have heard a very loud outcry against the Electoral College by the losing Democrats once again, regardless of the fact that they had well prevailed in the Electoral College in the two Obama elections of 2008 and 2012. Also, regardless of the fact that save for the ultra dark-blue state of California, President Trump won the popular vote of the aggregate other 49 states of the nation. And again, also regardless of the fact that California's vote majority by Democratic Hillary Clinton over GOP candidate President Trump was greatly fueled by California's very large Hispanic immigrant population-many of them illegals-and all were permitted to vote. President Trump's losing margin in the Western battleground states of Nevada and Colorado were much smaller than his 2016 margin of defeat in California though again the substantial Hispanic immigrant population in both states greatly contributed to his defeat in both, including by voting done by illegal immigrants, and other instances of Democratic vote fraud-particularly by the corrupt Democratic machine in Las Vegas, Nevada. However, the Electoral College as an American institution perseveres and continues on for as the Electoral College is a Constitutional provision in the US Constitution, it can only be eliminated or substantially changed by the amendment process to the US Constitution. As a result of Donald Trump's 2016 election, some Democrats have proposed to abolish the Electoral College and have proposed amendments to that effect which have since been introduced in Congress, the success of which are greatly open to question.

This Democratic effort to eliminate the Electoral College must be fully resisted by all GOP, conservatives, indeed, all liberty-loving Americans. The Electoral College protects the American Republic from leftist tyranny. The GOP is, and must remain, the perpetual guardian and protector of the Electoral College, and by implication, the liberties of the American Republics' citizens.

In the early 1970's at the time of massive re-election victory of President Richard M. Nixon-plus right after the publication of Kevin Phillips' Emerging Republican Majority-there was much Democratic angst that the Electoral College favored conservative Republican candidates. This was repeated somewhat, though with lessened intensity after the disputed 2000 Presidential Election very narrowly won by the Republican candidate (former) President George W. Bush over the Democratic candidate (former) Vice President under President Bill Clinton, Al Gore. However, the 2008 Presidential Election handily won by Democrat Barack Hussein Obama with a large Electoral College majority-fueled by the Demographic changes in the American political landscape described herein-now gives rise to legitimate Republican and conservative fears that the Electoral College now tilts to favor the Democratic left in Presidential Elections,

Bill Bennett, the popular conservative radio talk show host and former administrator in previous Republican Administrations with titles such as "Drug Czar," and Secretary of Education to his resume, has been heard to lament from his popular morning radio show, "Morning in America," the existence of the "Blue Block" of states in the Electoral College totaling 245 Electoral Votes which now consistently vote for the Democratic Presidential candidate-and have now for the last several Presidential Elections. And which states are these? Well, surprise, surprise, most are the states that I have both repeatedly mentioned and described, i.e.. States such as California, New York, Illinois, New Jersey, Massachusetts, Connecticut, Rhode Island, Vermont, etc.

Bennett's observation that this "Blue Block" of states is for the most part firm, and that in a typical Presidential Election all of the states comprising the Blue Block will support the Democratic Presidential candidate is essentially correct. This "Blue Block" of repetitive Democratic voting states in Presidential Elections now constitutes the alter-ego of the Kevin Phillips model of the regularly-voting Republican states in Presidential Election years located in the South, Mid-West, and the Mountain-West. Since this "Blue Block" of states according to Bennett comprises a floor of 245 Electoral Votes-again just 25 Electoral Votes short of victory for the Democratic candidate-the Republican Presidential candidate in a typical Presidential Election year has little margin for error. The Republican Presidential candidate must prevent at all costs the Democratic candidate from winning the additional 25 state Electoral Votes beyond the Democrat's "Blue Block" base of 245 Electoral Votes, or else the Democratic candidate will win. This is a most daunting feat and challenge for any Republican Presidential candidate in any Presidential election year.

In the 4 Presidential Elections of: 2008, 2004, 2000, and 1996-only former President Bush in both 2000 and 2004 managed to win

the 270+ Electoral Votes and deny victory to his Democratic opponent. However, in both instances, Bush's respective Democratic op-
ponents: Al Gore in 2000, and John Kerry in 2004 won an excess of
Electoral Votes beyond their 245 "Blue Block" (267 won by Gore in
2000; 252 won by Kerry in 2004). In 2016, Democrat Hillary Clinton
won but 227 electoral votes. With the small margin for error in the
Electoral College available for Republican candidates in Presidential
Elections due to the Democratic "Blue Block," the Democratic far
left which drives the Democratic Party-realizing how near to national
victory that they are in each Presidential election due to their "Blue
Block-" are emboldened to drive their far-left socialistic legislative
agenda as introduced by President Obama in 2009.

President Bush's successful 2004 Re-election campaign repeatedly boasted that it was playing ball on the Democratic "side of the
field" by repeated visits by both President Bush and his Vice President, Dick Cheney, into many of the Democratic "Blue Block" states,
states such as Pennsylvania (again, a soft Blue/tossup state), Michigan (another soft Blue state), New Jersey, and even Hawaii-both hard-
Blue states-in a spirited, determined effort to capture these states in
the election. In 2016, President Trump adopted the same strategy
of playing offense on the Democratic side of the field and did so
with great success. The 2012 Mitt Romney GOP campaign did also
attempt to do the same as Bush and Trump, but without the same degree of success. This effort unfortunately was ultimately unsuccessful
as Bush's Democratic opponent, Senator John Kerry, did capture all
of his 245 "Blue Block" Electoral Votes plus an additional 7 for a
total of 252 Electoral Votes. President Trump in 2016 made a particularly determined effort to smash through the Democratic "blue
Block" of states and seize some for his own and at last was the first
GOP candidate since 1988 successful in doing so, winning the states
of Pennsylvania, Michigan, and Wisconsin. Hillary Clinton, his Democratic opponent, only amassed 227 electoral votes. Trump's popular vote majorities in all of these states were not substantial (Pennsylvania's approximately 68,000; Wisconsin approximately 28,000;

and Michigan only approximately 12,000). Yet win them regardless, Trump did, and in so doing, taking a large chunk of the "Democratic Blue Block." A vigorous, effective program such as building a Red State Nation will expand the GOP majorities in these and other tossup states and transform them into red states for many elections to come.

Just as did President Trump in 2016, the President Bush 2004 Re-election campaign made a particular determined effort to capture the Electoral Votes of Pennsylvania, a Blue Block state having supported the Democratic presidential candidate in every election from 1992. Much advertising, resources, and repeated candidate visits were expended in this effort. Pennsylvania though a "Blue Block" state is nonetheless a "Weak Blue"/tossup state as illustrated by the 2004 Bush campaign effort there. President Bush though unsuccessful in 2004 in capturing Pennsylvania's 21 Electoral Votes, did come close, winning 49% of the state's popular vote. This is not insignificant in a state with the 2-bookend large Democratic cities of Pittsburgh and Philadelphia; powerful unions, and a legacy of Democratic corruption-particularly in Philadelphia.

Likewise in President Obama's successful 2008 election effort, his campaign expended much effort in traditional Republican states such as Colorado, Virginia, North Carolina, Indiana, Ohio, Nevada, and Florida-all of which were won by President Bush just 4 years before. Obama won all of these traditionally Republican states, plus others, in addition to his "Blue Block" Electoral College base to comprise his significant 2008 Electoral College victory (365 Electoral Votes). As both of these elections illustrate, the dominant party in an ascendancy-year election-Republican Party ascendancy in 2004; Democratic party ascendancy in 2008-that dominant party can aggressively pursue and seek to capture the Electoral Votes of states traditionally associated with the opposing party and may do so with some success. However, that success is generally confined to capturing the Electoral Votes of states weakly associated with the other party. The 2004 Bush Re-election campaign expended little effort or resources to attempt to win such Dark Blue/strong Democratic states as California, Illinois, New York, or Massachusetts. Likewise, the 2008 Obama effort-successful as it was-expended little effort or resources to win such Bright Red/strong Republican states as Alabama, Mississippi, Louisiana, and several states in the Mountain West and Great Plains (Wyoming, Utah, Nebraska, Kansas, etc.).

Presidential campaigns (successful ones anyway) are generally managed and run just as any successful, responsible, business and family household in America: they expend resources in a manner which represents the greatest possible return. The problem for American conservatives, the national Republican Party, the nation as a whole-and indeed, the purpose for this book-is that many of the largest states in this country: again, California, New York, Illinois, New Jersey, etc. in addition to being "Dark Blue" Democratic states, also include several of the largest, most populous states in the nation (California being of course, the largest). It is the high individual Electoral Vote totals from these states-particularly California- which give the Democratic Party such a current advantage in the Electoral College.

Three trends and developments leading up to the 2008 Presidential Election; the election itself with Obama's resulting victory; and its aftermath paint a clear picture: first, America through changes in its demographics is gradually evolving into a majority nonwhite nation. Secondly, the majority of the Democratic Party supporters in this nation support the implementation of a radical-leftist/socialist domestic political agenda. And third, if a contemporary Democrat such as Obama is elected President-particularly with a Democratic majority in both Houses of Congress as he enjoyed at the start of his Term in 2009-such a President will seek to enact just such a radical-leftist/socialist domestic political agenda. And again, the Democratic left's "Blue Block" in the Electoral College makes the left's socialist agenda a real risk for the nation, and a distinct possibility.

This is the threat to the Republic; to the traditional America that all of us have ever known-of allowing the national Democratic party to gain control of our national government which in 2009, it had (ie. Both Houses of Congress, plus the Presidency). What is the solution for both American conservatives and the Republican Party to combat the Democratic Party's advantages both in demographics and their Electoral College, "Blue Block?" Easy! The solution is Red State Nation! The Democrats' 245 Electoral College "Blue Block" can be attacked by simply, "lancing the boil," the same as removing any developing infection. As I have consistently emphasized here throughout, American conservatives have the power as free American citizens to both control their own destiny, and that of the nation by virtue of their own actions. They can do so by their vote; both at the ballot box and also with their feet. The Democratic "Blue Block" can be attacked by American conservatives and Republicans by their physically removing themselves from Blue Block states, and to cease contributing to the power of the Blue Block. If a conservative and Republican exodus from the states comprising the Democratic "Blue Block" can be initiated and maintained-a "Red State Nation" effect-the power and strength of their "Blue Block" will be steadily lessened, and the threat to the nation from entrenched socialistic Democratic power will steadily decrease as well.

I cannot underemphasize his point-which is the central theme of this effort here of mine- and that is that conservatives (especially) and Republicans in general have no business residing in such hard Democratic states such as especially California, New York, Illinois, and Massachusetts. They must and should move to more politically compatible states where their collective political power merged with the conservatives and Republicans already residing in those states, will magnify the force and strength of their vote, and contribute to the political health of the nation in the struggle against Democratic socialism. Conservatives and Republicans remaining in hard left and Democratic (and again, inevitably high-tax) states such as California, New York, Illinois, and Massachusetts-even if they consistently vote in these states-do nothing to improve their own individual political welfare and by remaining, actually harm the nation by contributing to the strength of the Democratic Electoral College "Blue Block."

Conservatives and Republicans remaining in these Democratic states are inevitably contributing to the propping up of rotting, failing, high-tax, hard-left and socialistic Democratic political structures. Remove the responsible, productive, tax-paying Republicans and conservatives from these states-or hopefully many of them anyway-and perhaps you kick the props out from some of these states which causes them to crash, and hopefully starts them on a long, painful road to reform which may eventually transform them into conservative, Republican, "Red" states themselves. The nation as a whole can only benefit from this process in the long run.

CHAPTER 6:

WHAT CAN I DO?
RED STATE DEMOCRATS AND RECALL.

So, what can American conservatives and Republicans do to participate, get involved, in this effort to fight socialism and combat the Democratic left for the future and political control of America? Many of the suggestions are common sense and oft-repeated. Stay involved on the issues (watching Fox News as I do every day is an excellent way to start). Contact your Representatives and US Senators to voice your conservative perspective on the critical issues of the day. Even if you reside in one of the "Dark Blue" states and your Senators and/or Representative happens to be a leftist, contact them anyway! Their staff that you speak with may not be particularly forthcoming to your views, but do not let that deter you. Your Representatives and Senators-leftists or not, and in pursuit of an ideological agenda-still work for you. Also, contribute to, volunteer for, and participate in-conservative causes-not the least of which is the Tea Party Movement. Lastly, vote in every election, primaries, and general elections. And vote conservatism, and for conservative candidates.

And remember, voting also means that in 99+% of the time, that means do not vote for a Democrat-any Democrat-no matter how conservative a particular Democrat may claim to be. Any candidate who receives campaign contributions through a political party and shares that political party designation of a "D" next to their name shares the same party designation as Barack Hussien Obama, Harry Reid, and Nancy Pelosi-socialists and leftists all, and therefore cannot be trusted. Lastly, always remember per the central thesis of this effort that conservatives can-and should vote with their feet, and not just in a ballot box and voting booth. Ten, a hundred, a thousand or even more conservative votes cast are worth far more in Red states such as Alabama, Mississippi, or Texas than if they are cast in Illinois or New York. This is especially so if the Red states' conservative voters previously lived in Blue states such as Illinois and New York and moved "Red" in order to vote-and live "Red," and in so doing, also contributing to a non-socialist, more prosperous, and safe America.

During much of 2009 in President Obama's first year in office, those resisting the enactment and imposition of his aggressive, socialistic legislative agenda-particularly the Obamacare Health Care Bill-frequently had their backs to the wall attempting to fight off the agenda despite the Democrats' large majorities in both Houses of Congress. In the US Senate where the Democrats had a filibuster proof majority of 60 senators for nearly all of 2009, it became evident that many of them represented essentially conservative, usual-Republican or Red states while at the same time voting to enact Obama's far-left legislative agenda with impunity-"independent " voting to be sure, at its finest.

In many instances, courageous though perhaps foolish-some of these Democratic senators were slated to face re-election in the November 2010 mid-term elections such as Blanche Lincoln in the state of Arkansas where it was presumed that an outraged conservative citizenry would promptly retire her, but what about the others? Research indicated that several Democratic senators who voted to support Obama's agenda-and who were not up for re-election in 2010-nonetheless represented Red states which had a provision which enabled them to face recall elections in their states should the state's voters force them to do so. However, there has only been one previous attempt to recall a US Senator, and that was the attempted, yet unsuccessful recall of the (late) liberal Democratic Senator Frank Church from the conservative (now Red) Mountain West state of Idaho by his then disaffected conservative voters. There are at present 18 states which permit recall elections for elected state officials. They are Alaska, Arizona, California, Colorado, Georgia, Idaho, Kansas, Louisiana, Michigan, Minnesota, Montana, Nevada, New Jersey, North Dakota, Oregon, Rhode island, Washington, and Wisconsin-many of these are "Red" states.

A particularly well-known recall election was in California in 2003 when the state's voters recalled existing Democratic Governor Gray Davis in favor of former action movie star and champion bodybuilder, Republican, Amold Schwarzenegger, who was re-elected in 2007 and remained Governor to this day in 2009. Several of the above-cited "recall" states which are also "Red" states had incumbent Democratic US senators who voted for Obama's 2009 left-wing legislative agenda-particularly the very unpopular Obamacare Health Care Law. Some of these particular Red state Democrats voted for Obama's agenda presumably felt that they were safe in doing so as they did not face their voters in a 2010 mid-term election as Blanche Lincoln of Arkansas did, even though they nonetheless represented both a Red, as well as a recall state.

One issue that should be explored by conservative voters and residents in individual "Red" states with Democratic US Senators-especially those states with US Senators not up for re-election in the next immediate election-is to recall their Democratic US Senator. In a situation such as the very unusual one which prevailed in 2009 with a left-wing, socialistic domestic agenda being crammed down the throats of the majority conservative voters in Red states, assisted by an elected Democratic US Senator of their state, why cannot serious recall movements be launched in these states which permit it to facilitate the removal of these Democratic senators? Clearly these senators in these specific "Red" conservative states in supporting Obama's agenda, cannot be said to represent the best interests of their constituents. Laws of individual states that permit for recall of elected officials should have perhaps been more explored and utilized for instance by those Red state conservative voters whose Democratic US Senators voted in support of the passage of Obamacare (Obama's socialist program of health care reform) in the US Senate in 2009.

All Democratic US Senators-not just those in the Red states-voted in favor of the passage of Obamacare. One Red state example of those Democratic US Senators who did this-US Senator Ben Nelson of Nebraska-supported President Obama's socialized medicine program in contravention of both the clear and expressed wishes of his own constituents, and of the national interest as well. Are some-if not all of these instances of these Red State Democrats-an example of "Profiles in Courage" per the famous book by John F. Kennedy? Perhaps! However, the flip side of one having "Profiles in Courage" is one having to take-and face-the consequences of their own actions. It must not be forgotten that most of the good conservative Red state voters in 2009 who had for whatever reason, previously elected a Democratic Us Senator to represent their state, did not do so for this senator to march in lockstep with a first-term Democratic President from Chicago's South Side; a President with both a far-left background and a history of like associations. This was also a President who was both the author and cheerleader of a far-left legislative agenda as befitting of both his background and associations. Those Red states which provided for recall, and whose Democratic US Senators voted for Obamacare in 2009 and ultimately in 2010 and who faced re-election in the 2010 mid-term elections clearly did not need to face a recall election in their individual states.

However, if serious recall movements were launched in those Red states with Democratic senators who did not face re-election in 2010 but which permitted recall, in addition to the many states, Red and otherwise, in which Democratic US senators would face re-election in 2010, the playing field would become uncomfortably large-and much more difficult-for the national Democratic Party to protect all of their contested US Senate seats, and it could undoubtedly have been overwhelmed and lose many of them. Even those Democrats who would successfully stave off a recall effort would do so by expending unplanned resources which would then not be available for when that same senator ran for re-election 2 or 4 years later. Likewise, resources expended by the national Democratic Party to protect and support one or more of their Red state senators facing a serious recall effort, would then be resources then unavailable to the Democratic Party to assist those Democratic senators facing normal re-election in 2010. Forcing the Democratic Party to expend precious limited resources to defend the seats of Democratic senators in Red states facing recall elections-plus those of the Democratic senators in other states facing normal elections-should seriously overtax the national Democratic party and should result in additional Democratic US Senate seats lost, and a greatly-weakened Democratic Party. Perhaps even the national Tea Party movement-either alone, or in conjunction with the state Republican Party in the individual Red and recall states-could seize the initiative of a recall effort in the individual states. However as always, conservatives in the individual states can as always, decide what is best for themselves.

As we repeatedly witnessed in 2009 and early 2010, conservative voters in legitimate "Red" states such as Nebraska, Arkansas, Louisiana, North Dakota, and Montana, etc. should not have to endure the indignity of having their elected representative-Democrat or not-vote in support of such programs as Obamacare and abortion on demand paid for by US tax dollars. When that happens, state law should ideally provide a recall remedy to these aggrieved conservative voters in these states, and that recall remedy ideally should be utilized. In any event, voters in Red states-particularly the dominant conservative ones-should remember this example of Democratic US Senators from their states voting in support of such programs as Obamacare and abortion and accordingly never forget that any Democrat, no matter how seemingly likeable, pragmatic, or even conservative, is nonetheless not to be trusted-or certainly voted for.

Hopefully, this Obama experience and this nation's close brush with socialism in 2009-2010 because Obama and his Democratic party were faced with-and took full advantage of-60 Democratic US Senators (the minimum filibuster-proof majority) including many from the Red states will teach once and for all the fool hardiness of majority Red state voters to vote for a Democratic US Senator to represent them. That includes any Democrat-no matter how seemingly independent, attractive, or conservative the Democratic Senate candidate appears to be-they simply cannot be trusted. The Obama "experience" clearly teaches us all that a Democratic US Senator representing any state is either a socialist himself or herself (albeit perhaps a closet socialist), or at the minimum, an "enabler" of socialism (for the right price!). It matters not, as we can afford none of them. The results of a poll announced on the Fox News Channel in early February 2010 announced that better than 30% of Democratic voters had a favorable view of socialism. That percentage is far higher today in 2020. Undoubtedly in specific states, particularly the darkest Blue states from which a Red State Nation project would draw the most émigrés from, that 30% pro-socialism figure among current Democratic residents may even be higher. Drawing large amounts of conservative and Republican émigrés from darkest Blue states such as California, Illinois, and New York will result in these already darkest Blue states becoming even more dark Blue, though less populous.

Some significant mid-cycle elections have taken place in recent years; chiefly the Fall. 2009 elections for governor in both the states of New Jersey and Virginia, and the special election for US Senator in Massachusetts in January 2010 to fill the seat of the late Democratic Senator, Ted Kennedy, upon his passing. All of these elections were won by the Republican candidate, and all were seen in varying degrees as a repudiation of Barack Obama and his Presidency. Particularly with the election of Republican Governor Chris Christie in New Jersey and Republican US Senator Scott Brown in Massachusetts, the question can logically be asked if the fundamental premise of this writing is wrong, i.e.. If it is really necessary for any for Republican and conservative voters to abandon residing in overwhelmingly Democratic and dark Blue states such as New Jersey and Massachusetts, and to concentrate their numbers-as well as Republican and conservative electoral strength-in other and friendlier states such as tossup states, and states that are already legitimate "Red" states, or Republican/conservative majority states. And while I certainly applaud the elections of these Republican candidates in these elections as does any other true Republican or conservative, Yes, I do think that the movement and concentration of Republican/conservative electoral strength as called for to stimulate a Red State Nation, is still necessary-even despite these thrilling Republican victories.

It should not be forgotten that these Republican election victories-particularly in New Jersey and Massachusetts-were again off-cycle elections in non-Presidential election years. In Presidential elections, New Jersey and Massachusetts consistently rate as two of the Bluest states in the Democrats' 245 Electoral Vote "Blue Block" The overwhelming Democratic nature of these 2 states truly becomes evident during Presidential elections when so much more of the Democratic majority base of these states becomes motivated and energized to vote in them as opposed to lesser elections in off-cycle years. Nothing was suggested by the results from those two elections in particular that the overwhelming Democratic nature in both New Jersey and/or Massachusetts has been altered, and that they remained overwhelmingly Democratic/dark Blue states in which whose voters simply sent an anti-Obama warning shot across the bow with the results of these two off-cycle elections. Indeed, in Massachusetts, when Scott Brown did run for re-election in 2012, he lost his Massachusetts US Senate seat to Democrat Elizabeth Warren, who rapidly gained the earned reputation as one of the US Senate's most pronounced leftists. Brown lost in 2012, a presidential election year, because the Massachusetts motivated Democratic voter base came out to vote in a very dark-blue state to support Obama and overwhelm GOP candidate Mitt Romney as well as Brown. To have survived and retain his US Senate seat beyond the 2012 election would have taken an enormous effort by Brown-a much greater one than his initial one needed to win the seat in the first place in January 2010. To have done so in overwhelming Democratic Massachusetts, Brown would have had to induce an extraordinary amount of ticket-splitting by Democrats who would have presumably already voted to re-elect their candidate for President, Barack Obama. Brown was ultimately unsuccessful in his quest for re-election to the US Senate in 2012. He can be seen from time to time as a special guest on the Fox News Channel. He can take small consolation that he ran far ahead in Massachusetts of the GOP Presidential candidate, Mitt Romney, the former GOP governor of the state. Meanwhile as of this writing, Elizabeth Warren who deposed Brown from his Senate seat is one of the several leftist Democratic for President in 2020 competing for the opportunity to run opposite President Trump.

My central premise again is that yes Massachusetts is an overwhelming Democratic majority state, and as such is a prime candidate for its Republican and conservative citizens to be induced to join the Red State Nation effort.

CHAPTER 7:

SECESSION AND NULLIFICATION.

The Obama Presidency has spurred a strong counter-reaction among conservative Americans, most of which has manifested itself into the large and growing Tea Party movement. However conservative militancy against the Obama Presidency has manifested itself in other ways as well-both as adjuncts to the Tea Party movement, and as separate from it as well. One particular unsettling trend in reaction to Obama's Presidency is a slow but steady uptick in activity in the 21 Century version of American secession discussion again as in the mid-19" Century, which of course culminated in the 11 Southern states forming the old Souther Confederacy and ultimately, the resulting American Civil War. What these modern-day secessionists may lack in numbers, they perhaps make up for in volume. MSNBC conservative commentator, Pat Buchanan, recently wrote an online article for Human Events on the subject of the increase of secessionist thought in response to the Obama Presidency. Republican Texas Governor Rick Perry, governor of a conservative state in which anti-Obama and anti-federalism ferment is particularly strong, pointedly reminded the US Government to not usurp the rights of the individual states as guaranteed in the 10" Amendment in the US Constitution. Not well-publicized though was the 2009 order issued by President Obama to the US Armed Forces, partially perhaps in response to the massive, national growth of the

Tea Party movement in response to his Presidency. Obama's order to the American military was to be alert, and to promptly respond to actual attempts of uprising against the US Government.

Additional rumblings were heard from the State of Texas during the course of the 2016 Presidential Campaign that the State of Texas would not accept a victory by Democratic candidate, Hillary Clinton. On the other hand, once President Trump secured his victory in the 2016 Campaign, in the midst of the various Democratic riotings and demonstrations against his victory, what received limited scrutiny was the announcement of a secession movement in its infancy in the dark blue state of California in reaction to Trump's election. So, secession as a subject and topic is one that is very much still with us and has been for a long time and is one never far from our consciousness.

It is not rare to find on conservative internet blogsites, individual posters who blog to advocate the principle of secession as a remedy, usually and specifically once again the secession of individual Southern states from perceived, big, pro-national government, liberal, Northern states (essentially again, Red state vs. Blue). Frequent pro-secessionist arguments hold forth that if secession were permitted and became a reality and conservative, Red, and Southern states would be permitted to remove themselves, the remaining big spending, Northern liberal states such as New York would spend themselves into oblivion, and within a short period of time would petition to rejoin the seceded states for financial assistance. I am not an advocate for, or a believer in, the pro-secessionist argument. Indeed, I am disturbed by it, and by the extent of it, and I recognize that it is a natural by-product of the Obama Presidency and its many and various socialistic schemes. Indeed, I am a strong advocate of the Northern and Union perspective in the US Civil War, a subject of which I am well versed, and have read many books over the years.

In addition, I as the author of this effort and also the advocate of a "Red State Nation" to insure conservative ascendancy in the United States, the Federal Government, and specifically the Electoral

College, am a product and native of Pennsylvania-one of the "liberal" Northeastern states that contemporary secessionists would most like to remove themselves from. The stereotype of Pennsylvania as a "liberal Northeastern State" is a highly-flawed one. Pennsylvania in the 2016 Presidential Election did go for Donald Trump, as did both the state House of Representatives and the State Senate did go for the GOP-by a large margin. Indeed, much of Central, Northern, and Western Pennsylvania is highly rural, conservative, and votes GOP. The only real "liberal "area of the state is the southeaster section consisting of the City of Philadelphia, and most of the 4 suburban counties which surround it. I do not believe that it is in any way contradictory to be both a conservative and also a (one nation) nationalist. I am profoundly moved by much about President Abraham Lincoln; particularly his excellent body of work in his writings that he has left to us; specifically in this instance on the subject of secession in his First Inaugural Address in 1861. His logic and clarity on the subject of secession in that address are inescapable, and when I encounter and discuss the subject of secession with one of its advocates, I always refer the individual to read-or re-read as the case may be-Lincoln's First Inaugural Address to become critically informed on the subject, and of its ramifications as a subject. It is certainly true as Lincoln stated in his Address that unlike a husband and a wife who separate, divorce, leave each other's company because they can no longer get along, different states and sections of the country cannot do this. They may-or may not-agree or get along, but what they cannot do is to leave each other's company.

Many contemporary conservatives-particularly those with a Southern perspective and/or background-still do not favor Lincoln or rate him highly on the scale of previous American Presidents. On a conservative internet website that I am a member of, Presidents Washington and Reagan rated far above Lincoln on an online poll of the most effective American Presidents. I do not agree with the consensus. If one subscribes to the contemporary conservative creed of preserving the concept of America as "the last best hope on earth," then first preserving the concept of America as an undivided-and indivisible-nation as Lincoln did, would seem to be paramount. I perceive a great incompatibility between the contemporary concept of a one-nation America being the "last best hope on earth," and a pro-secession/pro-Southern perspective on the American Civil War. I suspect that a great deal of the anti-Lincoln (and by incorporation), pro-secession/pro-Southern position on the American Civil War by some contemporary American conservatives is frustration by those conservatives on the current Red state/Blue state divide and stalemate in the American electoral process today. Many of these conservatives perhaps view and blame Lincoln for the forced union between conservative "Red" states today, and leftist/socialistic "Blue" states as an extension of his preserving by war a union of (former) slave and anti-slavery states (many of the same states) in his own time.

President Trump's contemporary conflicts with the modern Democratic Left's "resistance" including a partisan impeachment reminds one of President Lincoln's conflicts with Southern secessionists in the Civil War. The mutual hatred on both sides seems quite the same. I do not know why contemporary conservatives-however many there are-find favor with the flawed and discredited concept of secession-just as the Southern secession proponents did at the outbreak of the American Civil War. Modern day secessionists-and nullifiers (ie. advocates of nullification), are just as wrong and misguided-for many of the same reasons-as were the original Southern secessionists of 1861. It seems clear that the way today to wrest national political control from leftists and socialists who primarily reside in "Blue" states is best accomplished by a one-nation, national option such as a Red State Nation concept, rather than a 2-nation (or more) option which does nothing to reduce the proximity of the opposing Red states to Blue. Separating red States from Blue into separate adversarial Nations likely removes all possibility of accommodation and compromise which would exist and have Red state/Blue State adversarial relationship in a one-nation framework as at present.

As to the concept of nullification in principle, I am opposed to it as well for I do not believe that a specific state should be able to inform the US Government that a particular US law (or laws) are nullified or are null and void within the confines of said state. Nullification first became an important issue decades even before the Civil War in 1832 when the state of South Carolina informed the US Government that a tariff law which the State greatly objected to was rendered "null and void" within the borders of South Carolina. President Andrew Jackson at the time threatened military action against the state, and South Carolina-probably realizing the folly of individual state action against the US Government-quickly backed down while their Southern neighbors looked on. The episode was but a minor dress rehearsal for the 1860-1861 secession crisis precipitated by Abraham Lincoln's election as President in 1860. This crisis was again initiated by South Carolina, whose secession in December 1860 was rapidly followed over the next two months by the secession of six other Southern states. Following that in 1861 in near rapid succession was the formation of a rival Confederate States government; the Confederates firing on Fort Sumter in Charleston, South Carolina harbor; President Lincoln's call for Northern troops; the rapid secession of four more Southern states to join the Southern Confederacy; and lastly, the actual onset of the American Civil War.

With the triumph of the Union in the American Civil War, Federal supremacy over the individual states was presumed acknowledged and unchallengeable, and the terms nullification and secession faded by the most part into America's subconscious (save perhaps for some Southern bitter-enders). However, with the advent of Obama's Presidency in 2008 and his aggressive far-left national agenda, the terms nullification and secession have once again reappeared-and among many in the American conservative movement, have taken on a new urgency. Also, the Donald Trump GOP election in 2016 has stimulated among leftists, particularly in the state of California an interest and an examination of the terms of nullification and secession. The Democrat leader of the California state legislature warned after Trump's election that California is a sanctuary state which would protect the status of illegal alien residents of California. In addition, at the same time, the issue of California seceding from the union over primarily the issue of illegal immigration and federal opposition to the sanctuary status of illegals in California began to be discussed in the California legislature. Also, specific large cities across the nation such as New York, Chicago, Philadelphia-among many others-reiterated their sanctuary status to illegal immigrants against any adverse action taken by the incoming Trump Administration. By these actions, the Democratic Party has made clear that the illegal immigrant population in the United States is a very important voting constituency.; for the Party-quite possibly the most important one-and one which they will protect at all costs. Again, I do not believe in-or advocate for-either of the concepts of nullification or secession. Neither was anticipated or planned for in the US Constitution by the Founding Fathers, and so accordingly they can be deemed to be extra-Constitutional concepts.

If the American people-and particularly American conservatives-protect their liberties and not again take them for granted, we need never again fear that a radical socialist such as Barack Hussein Obama would be Constitutionally elevated to the US Presidency-much less with the overwhelming majorities of his fellow far-left Democrat playmates in both Houses of Congress-ready and willing to perform much more socialistic mischief. If we protect our liberties by voting regularly-both in ballot box, and as applicable with our feet as I have advocated herein-there will be no need to discuss such concepts as nullification and secession, and these concepts can once again be relegated to the dust bin of US history where they properly belong.

For those contemporary conservatives who are sympathetic to a pro-secession argument-be they involved in the Tea Party movement or not-simply because of their disgust with both the composition-and performance of our national government in Washington, D.C. between 2008-2010, I say give America a chance.; she is deserving of one. Even during the American Civil War, most Confederates-including their leaders-regularly paid homage to George Washington, and the rest of our Founding Fathers. In their wisdom, the Fathers constructed the Federal system under which we still live today. It is anticipated that most pro-secession conservative advocates are the way that they are out of extreme frustration because they believe that the United States as both a democratic concept as well as a Constitutional republic no longer functions, and obviously is no longer worth trying to fix-that is simply not true.

Conservatives, even secessionists, in different parts of the country have legitimate reasons to feel aggrieved at the seeming preponderance of left-wing political domination of many of the states-several of them large (California, New York, of course)-in certain sections of our It must be recalled that this left-wing political domination of these particular states translates into the "Blue Block" of 245 Electoral votes in the Electoral College. However, consistent with the words and analysis of Lincoln, secession is not-and never was-a realistic alternative to serious political differences in this country. To the contemporary secessionists who grew upset by both the actions and socialistic course of the Obama Presidency, and the Blue Block Democratic states which elected him-and to date have largely sustained him and his actions-contemplation of secession is now no more of a realistic solution than it was in the days of Lincoln and the Civil War.

Instead, the best solution to insure to seriously damage the Democratic left's Blue Block of Electoral Votes, and to keep the Democratic left from achieving national political power and domination is a program advanced here such as Red State Nation. This program which provides for the expanded concentration of conservative and Republican voters in their own dominant states, and which in turn ultimately translates to a consistent electoral majority of Electoral Votes in the Electoral College. In the electoral combination of states to build and maintain a consistent coalition of conservative political power, ie. A Red State Nation-and to deny power once again to the American Democratic left-the 11 states of the old Southern Confederacy in the Civil War are of vital importance to this endeavor. That is why I oppose in principle the concept of secession, both now and in the past. It is now all hands-on deck! This nation needs all of its conservative and Republican-leaning states to remain in the fold in order to deny political power to-and defeat the socialistic schemes of-the Democratic left, who if permitted as already seen during Obama's Presidency, would radically change this nation from what it has heretofore been.

An effort towards a Red State Nation must construct-and consistently maintain-a political model in which it can consistently win elections, and elect conservatives as President every 4 years. To attempt otherwise such as secession would be to attempt to both repudiate Lincoln and the essence of democracy. Lincoln himself said many times during the American Civil War that the purpose for the War was to prove that popular government did not prove to be an absurdity. He also did not wish to see losers resort to bullets and rebellion to attempt to achieve and obtain political power when they could not achieve it by the election results itself. Red State Nation as a pro-one nation effort and as such, is entirely contradictory to secession and is compatible to both Lincoln and democracy. The years of President Trump's first term, 2017-2020 can be described as a "non-hot" or non-shooting, civil war. Prior to Trump's Inauguration, Democrats were already planning his impeachment. The first part of his term consisted of a period of Democratic resistance, culminating in a partisan impeachment based upon political, non-criminal reasons.

Yes, America needs all conservative and Republican-leaning (ie. Red) states who if left unchecked might otherwise contemplate secession from the Union-particularly when presented with the prospect of a Presidency such as Obama's with a clear left-wing/socialistic domestic political agenda, plus his minority group status, his debatable citizenship status, and his Muslim heritage. America needs the combined electoral and political power provided by its conservative states in order to remain a conservative, center-right nation as a whole. On those occasions-thankfully rare-in American history when such an extreme Democratic President as Obama would ascend to the White House, he should be countered and checked by legal and constitutional means rather than by an utterly inappropriate process such as secession. Our Founding Fathers in their wisdom devised the present American political system as governed by the US Constitution with plenty of avenues for both self correction, and checks and balances. The Electoral College in its own right is one of those means of self correction, and conservatives and Republicans in this nation by concentrating their political power and relocating themselves to conservative -friendly "Red" states are very much self correcting the American political system.

All conservatives, Tea Party activists, and true Republicans in this nation-no matter where their state of origin: Maine, Idaho, Alabama, Alaska, or California-must vote and pull together in order to defeat Obama and his far-left Democratic Party, and its radical socialist agenda. Obama-and his designs-cannot be defeated if some conservatives do wish to fight him back and save freedom for this country and contest his march towards socialism, while others simply wish to jump into the lifeboats and flee. If an attempt would ever be made during Obama's Presidency-or beyond it during anyone's Presidency anytime during my lifetime-to again disrupt the permanency and security of this union of states in these United States of America, I would of course support the upholding of the Constitution of the United States of America and the maintenance of these union of states-yes even if the President would be Barack Obama. It would be very painful and uncomfortable for me to support any leftists Democratic President like President Barack Obama in any endeavor. It is-and would be-even more painful to witness Barack Obama wrap himself in the mantle of President Abraham Lincoln, any more than he already has.

As a firm American conservative, unalterably opposed to the American left and the Obama socialist agenda which they have spawned, I am equally opposed to the yearnings of those conservative neo-cons in both Texas, and other states-Southern and non-Southern-for a stress, hassle-free ability to simply leave Obama, leftists, socialism, high taxes, etc., behind by a simple, uncomplicated ability of individual states to secede from the United States. I sympathize, and very much so, with the impulse to leave Obama and all that he represents behind in simply voting to escape him in an act of secession. However, pleasing it may be though to contemplate secession, secession nonetheless as a concept is one that is idyllic, overly-simplistic, and very unrealistic. Red States are needed to fight Obama, and the American left, and to support and defend the cause of freedom and Constitutional government, and that is not possible if individual states view the American union as little more than a turnstile at a bus station.

Also, individual acts of secession such as individual acts of renouncing one's American citizenship and/or moving to another country to take up residence in order to escape Obama and the American left-such as famous conservative commentator Rush Limbaugh has repeatedly threatened to do-is always an individual option, but in my view at the present time is a premature one, at least on a mass, widespread scale. It is far easier, less expensive, and yes, more patriotic-for conservatives, Republicans, or any freedom-loving Americans of means opposed to far-left socialism and high taxes to move from say New York to Florida; Illinois to Kentucky; or California to Utah to work to build a Red State Nation than to move from their states of origin to foreign countries such as New Zealand, Australia, Switzerland, etc. It is however somewhat humorous to now witness several well-known movie and television stars-prominent leftists all-such as Cher, Whoopie Goldberg, Miley Cyrus, etc. to threaten to move to Canada in response to Donald Trump's election as President in 2016. I don't want to see freedom-loving, patriotic conservative Americans fleeing the country-or to contemplate doing so- any more than I want to see others agitate for secession. I do want to see-and we need-everyone working together to save this country from the Democratic left and socialism, and to preserve it as the "Last Best Hope on Earth."

All that is necessary to change this country for the better is to use the Constitutional mechanics to regain-and retain-control as our Founding Fathers have left to us-just as our leftist adversaries have done. Yes, again I mean the Electoral College. This country is worth saving and can indeed still be saved from the American left, by the united and determined resolve of all American conservatives. If anyone wants to flee the country, let the leftists mentioned previously do it. Let the leftists be the ones to attack the Electoral College. Conservatives must and should embrace, protect, and use the Electoral College and all other Constitutional mechanisms to to regain-and retain-political control, just as our Founding Fathers have passed down to us. Again, as to secession-prone or secession-inclined Red states, they must and shall be discouraged, and if necessary-withstood. We are all in this together-all Red states, North, South, East, and West-in this sacred struggle to preserve the Constitutional America of our Fathers from socialism and the American left, and it is again, all hands-on deck. We have none to spare for individual flights of fancy to again explore secession. Those secession advocates who remain today and who presumably advocate for it on the basis of upholding and defending the United States Constitution-just as those in the past; previous to and during the American Civil War-simply and foolishly fail to see -that the United States Constitution cannot be defended or enhanced by extra-Constitutional means and/or actions, and that to even try to do so is both foolish and unnecessary. Our system of government is one created by the collective wisdom of the Founding Fathers and is one that encourages change. Red State Nation as a concept is entirely consistent with the designs of the Founders. American citizens vote for change both in the ballot box, and with their feet. That page which is secession is yesterday's news and has already been turned. For better or for worse, we are-and will remain-one nation.

However unfortunate that it may be to many that Barack Obama was for a time of 8 years, President of the United States, the nation that he represents was, and still remains the last best hope for mankind as a symbol for freedom and justice on this earth. In our history, countless millions from other nations have struggled and died to reach these shores, and many others also have once they successfully arrived here. And of course, many Americans have likewise died-both here and in many foreign lands in America's many wars-in order to preserve unblemished this nation's symbol of freedom and justice. Obama but temporarily occupied the White House, and this nation has survived him, and other bad Presidents before. But the nation itself, must-and shall-endure.

CHAPTER 8:

THE ENTITLEMENT SOCIETY OF
THE AMERICAN DEMOCRATIC LEFT.

After his impressive electoral victory in 2008, Barack Hussein Obama has suffered a significant drop in approval. Many of his 2008 supporters evidently had experienced "buyers remorse" by 2012, even though he was re-elected in that year. Many more did experience "buyers remorse" by 2016 as evidenced by the election of Donald Trump. Obama may quite possibly turn into an aberration as President as I have speculated previously; a leftist radical-otherwise unelectable nationally-who won the US Presidency in the moment of a perfect storm by hitting a confluence of favorable events at the same time: facing a 2008 American electorate wearied by a greatly unpopular President of the other party; and unpopular war; and a fast-deteriorating economy. Hopefully, these are the conclusions-which will come to pass

However, even with the election of Donald Trump in 2016, a movement towards a conservative dominant nation -a Red State Nation-should still advance. The confluence of favorable events that allowed a socialist such as Obama with a large Democrat-majority Congress has already occurred once in 2008, with his re-election in 2012. It could just as easily happen again. The reactive nature inherent in popular democracies in general, and within the American political system in particular is good in many respects. A Presidency such as Obama's which arrived at the vanguard of favorable events and trends, can easily rapidly depart in the same manner-particularly if the unpopular events and trends which would speed its departure, the Obama Presidency itself was largely responsible for-such as say the George W. Bush Presidency which preceded his, being responsible for the very-unpopular Iraq War.

Barack Obama and his current version of the leftist national Democratic party represent and drive for the creation of a socialist America because they represent the aspirations of those millions of Americans who want to create and share in an entitlement society. When Obama in a near fatal slip of the tongue to "Joe the Plumber" in Joe's front yard in Ohio during the 2008 Campaign told Joe that he (Obama) wants to "spread the wealth around," Obama was preaching the gospel of America's entitles who want to transform America into socialism. It is open to speculation whether as some believe that Obama's vision to create a socialist entitlement society in this country is in reality his attempt to facilitate reparations for America's legacy of slavery. It is however quite feasible that many in Obama's far-left constituency-both black and white-have slavery reparations as a desired object of his socialistic, entitlement program. Though Obama in his 8-year Presidency made no effort to enact slavery reparations, several of the 2020 Democratic Presidential candidates voiced support for the concept.

The flip side-and perhaps even the darker side-of this vision of the entitlement American society which Barack Obama and his far-left constituency are attempting to create is a society based upon preferences. The changes are subtle in some instances-some instances not so subtle-but all are real, nonetheless. It is a society that is indifferent to-if not downright hostile to-enforcing our nation's laws with respect to illegal immigration because most of the illegal immigrants are poor, disadvantaged, have a darker ie. non-Caucasian) skin complexion, and are told to vote Democratic, and usually do so. We are also being conditioned to be indifferent to-if not downright hostile to-the idea of treating our nation's sworn enemies from radical Islam as enemies, regardless of the nature or severity of the acts of war or criminal acts by these enemies against this nation. Terrorists are no longer referred to as terrorists. Acts of terror are no longer referred to as such.; perpetrators of terrorist criminal acts against this nation-or against individual Americans-no matter how severe or heinous should be viewed with understanding if not outright sympathy because inevitably the terrorists too had a poor and disadvantaged background from their native country as well as a darker (non-Caucasian) skin complexion, and invariably America was cruel and unfair to them in the same way. Also, poor, disadvantaged muslim refugees must be allowed into the country by the tens of thousands, spread out throughout the entire country-concentrating on Red states-and must not be allowed to be properly vetted, including the disclosure of any online pro-terror postings. And pertaining to criminal acts by accused terrorists-regardless of their nation of origin, plus actual written US Law which permits otherwise-these terrorist suspects are mandated to receive by the Obama Administration all of the Constitutional protections enjoyed by any American citizen.

Lastly, the entitlement society and mindset represented and heralded by the Presidency of Barack Obama and his far-left socialistic constituency is unfortunately also manifesting itself in our legal system. The hope and expectation of a fair and even-handed American system of justice as represented at countless courthouses in America by the robed, blindfolded woman holding the scales of justice is becoming more speculative and open-to-question due to the growth of the Obama entitlement American society; its support of "preferences;" and its permeation into even the American legal system. The same principle applies there as in the previous cited examples. George Soros and his far-Left network are assisting in the election of district attorneys across the country who are refusing to prosecute smaller crimes, resulting in the deterioration of the quality of life. Again, the legal system ideal of the Obama entitlists holds that certain people based upon their background of poverty, racial and/or types of discrimination, are also entitles to "preferences"-and regardless of any resulting injustice to anyone else-many instances, glaringly so. In our legal system in recent years, one example in recent years is the spectacle of many people applauding the acquittal of OJ Simpson in his 1994-95 criminal trial for the murder of two people 6 one, his former wife), despite the seeming weight of the evidence supporting his conviction.

Another well-known case-and a continuing one is that of Mumia Abdul Jamar-a black man who was convicted of executing a Philadelphia, PA police officer, and who was sentenced to death in a Philadelphia courtroom. Jamar, a well-spoken, intelligent man initiated a popular movement among entitlists who were motivated by his piteous complaints that he did not receive a fair trial. This resulting groundswell on Jamar's behalf-an international one even-resulted in the PA Supreme Court reducing Jamar's sentence for the death penalty to life imprisonment. Lastly, another ongoing case as of this writing is a Missouri one which originated in 1991. It involves a black man named Reginald Clemons who formerly sat on Missouri's Death Row, convicted of the crime of rape and murder of two young white women and sisters. It is a particularly brutal and heinous case in which Clemons following following his participation in the rape of the sisters threw them naked to their deaths off a a St. Louis bridge into the Mississippi River over 50 feet below. Clemons and his three fellow accomplices in this unspeakable crime (2 other black men; I white man) were all convicted. One of the defendants also received the death penalty from the state of Missouri and was executed in 2005. Another defendant also received the death penalty, but it was later reduced to life imprisonment by the Missouri Legislature. The last defendant who did not participate in the rapes, and who testified against the other defendants, received a 30-year sentence, and was paroled after 15 years.

At one time, Reginald Clemons while on Missouri's Death Row and awaiting an execution date, had enlisted popular support-primarily in the St. Louis black community-much the same as OJ Simpson, and Mumia Abdul Jamar, did in the larger national community, as well as in their respective communities, though in this instance, Clemons' support to prevent his execution is mostly confined to the St. Louis black community. He has however received the support and assistance of such popular black figures-and Obama associates-as actor Danny Glover, and Nation of Islam leader, Louis Farrakhan. The other two black defendants in this case also enlisted and received popular support in the St. Louis black community; the one defendant while he still had a death sentence, and prior to his commutation to life imprisonment; and the second defendant also did prior to his execution in 2005.

A common pattern is emerging here as can be easily seen in all of these cited cases: OJ Simpson, Jamar, and the Clemons and other 2 St. Louis ones-all of which are capital cases (ie. murder). In all of them, the defendants invited, enlisted, and received support from the greater black community-and in some instances a wider net of support-as noted, this wider net of support largely included support from well-known left-wing circles and figures. The underlying, unstated principle in each of these cases-and in the many similar ones in recent years in the United States which I did not research or cite-is that black defendants in each of these cases were "entitled" to favorable consideration at the expense of their victims .Another example of this entitlement concept with respect to criminal activity is that of the nearby to St. Louis MO was the famous Ferguson MO riots several years later while Obama was President, and in which he involved himself which resulted from a young black male shot and killed by a white police officer after assaulting the officer and attempting to steal the officer's gun. In each case instance, a sort of "post-partum" reparations was presumed to be owed due to America's shameful past legacy of slavery, Jim Crow, and lynchings which American blacks had experienced in the past.

The current development in recent years of the Black Liver Matter movement is also consistent with the demands for entitlement to favorable consideration due to race. This national movement consists of members-not all of whom are black-who have organized in reaction to a perceived excess of black victims killed by police officers nationwide-particularly by white police officers. This Black Lives Matter movement is an anti-police movement and has participated in many anti-police demonstrations across the country. Its' members have participated in violent actions against police officers. Par for the course, President Obama has invited-and welcomed-Black Lives Matter to visit him at the White House, while Hillary Clinton reached out and embraced them during her 2016 Presidential campaign.

This entitlement leftist philosophy as witnessed in these cited examples of crimes committed involving black defendants and victims is witnessed much the same in discussions-particularly critical ones-on the subject of the Presidency of Barack Hussien Obama, itself. There is a significant viewpoint within the large portion of the liberal community which supports President Obama that he is entitled to govern devoid of excessive criticism-particularly criticism by whites and especially white conservatives, and that such an excess of criticism is presumed to be racially motivated, and not politically motivated. It must not be overlooked that a large minority of the white community-for the most part those of the liberal/left-share the entitlement perspective of Obama, and is for the most part, ardent supporters and advocates of the liberal black community and its goals. A look back at the Obama Presidency-particularly in lieu of the current effort by the leftist Democrats to impeach President Trump-is that Obama skated through his 8-year Presidency-replete with excesses and dubious legal actions (with some clear illegal ones), plus nearly non-stop corruption, and got away with nearly all of it. This is because most Republicans in Congress were greatly intimidated from even contemplating initiating against the country's first African-American President. Obama then had virtually free reign to do as he wished throughout his entire 8-year Presidency. And he did just that!

It is these liberal/left members of the white community who voted for Obama in 2008-in numbers significant nationwide to provide him with his margin of victory-in many instances simply because Obama was black and was therefore "entitled" to their vote for that reason alone more than the white Presidential candidate ,the deceased Republican John McCain. McCain had an established reputation as an otherwise nominally-progressive Republican candidate with a further reputation of reaching out to-and currying support from-Democrats. Also, it is hardly unusual to find whites of the liberal/left to participate, sign petitions, etc. in support of black defendants who had been fairly convicted of the most horrific crimes as already seen, again because the black defendants were black and as such were therefore entitled to increased consideration. As long as the ranks of the American liberal/ left are going to be swelled by a large minority of the white community (30-35%), as well as by much higher percentages in the different minority groups-whose percentages in the total population are also increasing due to changing demographics-the total conversion of the America we have heretofore known into a true socialistic, entitlement state draws ever nearer. Although one can hope that recent infant trends of slowly increasing black support for President Trump will continue for the betterment of the nation.

Leftist justice though frequently entitlement based, need not necessarily though be racially based. Consider the well-publicized case of 2016 Democratic nominee Hillary Clinton and the strings that were pulled given her widely suspected criminal involvement with both her email activity with a private computer service while United States Secretary of State, as well as her Clinton Charity Foundation. Clearly just to allow Clinton to run for President in the first place, a lot of coordination had to occur between President Obama, his Attorney General, Loretta Lynch, both Bill and Hillary Clinton, and FBI Director, James Comey. The personal and private meeting between Lynch and Bill Clinton on an airplane in the Phoenix Arizona airport, literally just days before FBI Director Comey announced that no charges would be sought against Hillary Clinton, greatly highlights this brazen and suspected coordination. Also to be noted that while Comey was on national television announcing the lack of charges to be filed against Hillary Clinton-President Obama and Hillary Clinton were in an airplane together enroute to a campaign event in North Carolina-tight coordination indeed! Only the war of attrition and stalemate-ie. trading rooks for pawns, etc.-with the American left in swapping Presidential elections for the last 20+ years, has kept the left at bay though not by much given that the Democratic left's "Blue Block" of states within the Electoral College with their 240+ Electoral Votes is less than 30 Electoral Votes short from the required 270 for victory. We conservatives cannot save this country and fight the Democratic left as we heretofore have done election by election-as we ultimately will lose due to the evolving demographics factor in their favor.

Once lost to a socialistic, entitlement state, this nation is ultimately altered forever. Republicans, conservatives, and those Americans who wish to resist the descent to a socialistic, entitlement state must roll the dice in the quest for a game changer in order to stop the left, and our gradual transformation into an entitlement, socialist society which they, the left, have engineered. This game changer is a Red State Nation national effort to concentrate Republican and conservative oriented voters into a firm block of individual states in the United States which total a consistent 270 Electoral Votes in the Electoral College; that is the goal! With this goal realized, conservatives and Republicans should consistently control most-if not nearly all-Presidential elections. Given the current demographic trends within the United States with the rate of population growth of the various non-Caucasian groups greatly outpacing that of the Caucasians-plus the firm 30-35% of Caucasians who would nonetheless support a leftist/socialist political agenda and vote Democratic-no other realistic "game changer" other than Red State Nation is evident., given the US Constitution's mandate of the use of the Electoral College in the election of US Presidents. Red State Nation empowers US conservatives of all races to save the country from the American left, and to control our national destiny. Again it must be emphasized that the salvation of the nation from the Democratic Left must include the riding of the wave of the nation's present demographic trend by conservative America to reach out to and include members from all racial and ethnic groups-as many as possible-as President Trump is doing. It is the country of all of us, and we cannot save it-Red State Nation or no-without them. The Red State Nation then is, must be, and will be a color-blind nation that respects and cherishes the unique qualities and positive contributions of all of her citizens: those who obey the law; pay their taxes; and likewise respects and honors their fellow citizens will be the cornerstone of the endeavor. We cannot have it otherwise. I have written plainly that the United States as envisioned and launched by our Founders will not survive the persistent assaults and undermining permeated by the socialist entitlists of the devious American Left, unless the Red State Nation prevails-which it will not do-without all hands-on deck: patriotic, conservative, Americans of traditional values-regardless of race, creed, nationality, etc. The GOP and the Red State Nation must and will be inclusive for all for this nation to survive. Let us join together to make that happen.

CHAPTER 9:

THE ELECTORAL
COLLEGE AND CONCLUSION.

As the Electoral College as an institution is a specific Constitutional provision in the US Constitution, it can only be eliminated or substantially changed by the amendment process to the US Constitution. The operation of the Electoral College in its function of selecting the President of the United States is spelled out in the Twelfth Amendment to the US Constitution as ratified in 1804. The Twelfth Amendment modified somewhat the operation of the Electoral College in its role of selecting the US President as originally devised by the Founding Fathers in Article 2, Section 1, Clause 3 of the US Constitution. There have been from time-to-time movements and efforts to modify and/or abolish the Electoral College and to transform the US electoral system, chiefly into a direct popular election of the President of the United States. There is even a movement at present to abolish the Electoral College. Despite the Democratic left's built in advantages with the Electoral College with their Blue Block of 240+ Electoral Votes, there is much support within the left to abolish the Electoral College, chiefly as the result of the 2000 Presidential Election of Republican President George W. Bush which required the US Supreme Court to resolve in which Democratic candidate, Al Gore, actually won the popular vote by a miniscule margin, but Bush won the Electoral Vote, and was thereby awarded the Presidency. Apparently some in the Democratic left seem to think that direct popular election of the US President gives them even more built-in advantages than their Blue Block does in the present Electoral College system. As again in this writer's view- and that of many others- that this is a center/right nation, the idea that direct popular election of the US President gives the Democratic left additional advantages is viewed by me with much skepticism. In any event, the debate-as well as the institution itself of the Electoral College-continues on.

Clearly the results of the 2016 Presidential Election in which Democratic Hillary Clinton won the popular vote by more than 2 million votes -mostly due to her massive margin of victory in California, consisting largely of the Mexican-American vote-many of them presumed to be illegal immigrants-will again fuel the calls to abolish the Electoral College.

It is unknown if the attempt to ultimately abolish the Electoral College will meet in the future with greater success than previous attempts in the past have done. The original goal by the Founding Fathers was for the Electoral College to give a greater significance to those smaller population states in the United States in the selection process of US Presidents. That is no less a credible goal today than it was when the Electoral College concept was first devised by the Fathers and inserted in the Constitution. As there are many more smaller population states today than in the original 13 states which existed at the outset of the US Constitution-and quite a few of them are Red states who would have to approve-it seems unlikely that the Electoral College will be substantially modified or abolished altogether anytime soon. I have written this effort to conservatives and Republicans to utilize the Electoral College in order to fashion a Red State Nation with the view of the permanence of the Electoral College as an institution in mind. Proof that the Electoral College works exactly as designed by the Founders is evidenced in the 2016 Presidential Election by the frequent attention paid to the small population states of New Mexico, Utah, and New Hampshire particularly by winning GOP candidate Donald Trump.

The boiler plate argument for the institution of the Electoral College in that election by the American people in Presidential elections of "electors" in the College rather than directly voting for the American President by a direct popular vote is necessary to give added weight to the importance of the smaller states, which otherwise would presumably be largely ignored by the major Presidential candidates in their attempt to win by concentrating their efforts to win in the larger, vote-rich states. Again, I do not in principle oppose the Electoral College in concept or as an institution, nor do I favor an attempt to replace it, or significantly alter it. Again, to attempt to do so would be a difficult event, most time consuming-and more than likely, prove to be a fruitless effort by those making the attempt as it could only be done by Constitutional Amendment.

However, I also do not fully accept-or agree with-the boiler plate argument that the Electoral College is a necessity to protect the interests of the smaller-population states, given the practical reality of how the last several American Presidential elections were both conducted, and ultimately resulted. In the last several Presidential elections, only approximately 10-13 of the 50 states were seriously contested between both the Democratic and Republican Presidential candidates. Furthermore, those 10-13 states are largely (though not entirely) confined to that swath of states in the middle of the country between Pennsylvania and Iowa, inclusive (ie. Pennsylvania, Ohio, Michigan, Wisconsin, Missouri, Minnesota, Iowa, etc.). Again, a typical liberal Democratic Presidential candidate in a Presidential election would rarely campaign or expend many resources in the attempt to win the Electoral Votes of say Alabama or Mississippi, and likewise a conservative Republican Presidential candidate would waste little effort or resources to win the Electoral Votes of New York and Vermont. Although New Hampshire is a very small state-and in most presidential elections is heavily contested-it has flipped from GOP to Democrat in recent elections. As already said, both the Democratic and Republican parties have both already benefited from the Electoral College as an institution in its present form. The Democratic Party has their Blue Block of 245 or so Electoral Votes, and the Republican Party has their contemporary electoral carry over of the old Kevin Phillips model from 1969 of states in the South, Mid-West, and Mountain-West. It could perhaps be suggested that both the national Democratic and Republican Parties have so benefited from the Electoral College as an actual institution that both Parties would be harmed by the demise of it.

The Democratic attempt in 2016 to derail Donald Trump's Presidency at the outset by attempted bribes, threats, and appeals to the electors to abandon voting to elect Trump in unique in American history. Such an attempt was never even attempted to Abraham Lincoln's electors and circumvent his Presidency, just prior to the outset of the American Civil War. Clearly with the Democrats brazen attempt to tamper with the electors of the legitimate winning Presidential candidate, something must be done to guard against that happening in the future. Federal legislation must be passed to protect against it, or possibly even protection by Constitutional amendment.

The continued stability of the American political system with respect to the election of the American President every four years suggests strong evidence that the Electoral College has worked well as the fixed instrument to facilitate that event. The issue then simply becomes how can American conservatives simply, consistently, and successfully navigate the 50-state American political landscape - and master the Electoral College in order to elect a conservative Republican as President of the United States. The answer is (again) by attempting to build an electoral model based upon a Red State Nation. Conservative, Republican America is simply in a personal-and high stakes-game of chess or if one would prefer) poker with the American Democratic left in order to achieve political power in this country, and for the right to set and define the political direction of the country. With respect to the election of the American President, the Electoral College sets and defines the "rules of the game."

We have already seen via the far-left Obama agenda what the election of a leftist President such as Barack Obama along with overwhelming Democratic majorities in both Houses of Congress, means. Unchecked power on such a scale in the US Government by the American Democratic left would mean socialism pure and simple in America, and the end of both freedom and the free enterprise American economic system as we have heretofore known it. We cannot afford for this to happen, so the Democratic left must be stopped. In particular, leftist Democrats such as Barack Hussein Obama must not be permitted to again win election to the American Presidency via garnering of a 270 Electoral Vote majority in the Electoral College. Again, the building-and maintaining by American Republicans and conservatives of a national electoral model to achieve political power based upon a Red State Nation is a true path to consistent, concentrated electoral power in the Electoral College, as well a consistent conservative and Republican electoral victory.

The Founding Fathers in their diligence and collective wisdom devised a political system that is well-constructed, self-sustaining, adaptable to change, and able to reflect the prevailing national will and sentiment via elections. The national will and sentiment as expressed by the American people by their votes can then be translated into immediate action to effect the national will, and to bring it to fruition. We as a people need to do nothing more than to properly utilize what the Fathers have left us; vote; participate in elections; utilize the Electoral College as an instrument to effect change-permanent conservative change to remove the threat to the nation of the American Democratic left. Red State Nation is but a means to do just that. Let us then save this Republic that our Founders bequeathed to us. Let us build the Red State Nation. Let us begin!

BIBLIOGRAPHY

SOURCE SUMMARY

1. The Emerging Republican Majority by Kevin Phillips

2. A Rip In Heaven by Janine Cummins

www.ingramcontent.com/pod-product-compliance
Lightning Source LLC
Chambersburg PA
CBHW071206130726
47998CB00002B/645